THE STRANGE ODYSSEY OF POLAND'S NATIONAL TREASURES, 1939–1961

GORDON SWOGER

THE STRANGE ODYSSEY OF POLAND'S NATIONAL TREASURES, 1939–1961

A Polish-Canadian Story

THE DUNDURN GROUP
TORONTO

Copy-Editor: Lloyd Davis
Design: Jennifer Scott and Andrew Roberts
Printer: University of Toronto Press

Library and Archives Canada Cataloguing in Publication

Swoger, Gordon
  The strange odyssey of Poland's national treasures, 1939-1961 / Gordon Swoger.

ISBN 1-55002-515-5

1. Art — Poland. 2. Art treasures in war — Poland — History — 20th century. 3. World War, 1939–1945 — Art and the war. 4. Cultural property — Protection — Poland — History — 20th century. I Title.

N7255.P6S88 2004   940.53'1   C2004-905469-4

1   2   3   4   5   08   07   06   05   04

We acknowledge the support of the Canada Council for the Arts and the Ontario Arts Council for our publishing program. We also acknowledge the financial support of the Government of Canada through the Book Publishing Industry Development Program and The Association for the Export of Canadian Books, and the Government of Ontario through the Ontario Book Publishers Tax Credit program, and the Ontario Media Development Corporation's Ontario Book Initiative.

Care has been taken to trace the ownership of copyright material used in this book. The author and the publisher welcome any information enabling them to rectify any references or credit in subsequent editions.

J. Kirk Howard, President

Printed and bound in Canada.
Printed on recycled paper.

www.dundurn.com

Dundurn Press
8 Market Street, Suite 200
Toronto, Ontario, Canada
M5E 1M6

Gazelle Book Services Limited
White Cross Mills
Hightown, Lancaster, England
LA1 4X5

Dundurn Press
2250 Military Road
Tonawanda NY
U.S.A. 14150

*I would like to dedicate this book to my 3IB and 4IB History classes
at Nicholas Copernicus High School in Warsaw, 1994–95,
whose enthusiasm and interest got this Polish-Canadian
connection off to a great start.*

*And to my wife, Barbara, and our children,
who never doubted that the project would be carried through
to a successful conclusion.*

TABLE OF CONTENTS

MAPS

These maps were prepared by Suzanne
Dodge and Associates Inc.

347 Centre Street, P.O. Box 1839
Prescott, Ontario, K0E 1T0
tel: 613-925-4665
email: ssdodge@sympatico.ca

MAP I - Poland in 1939/Escape Route

POLAND'S FRONTIER

MAP II - Poland 1025

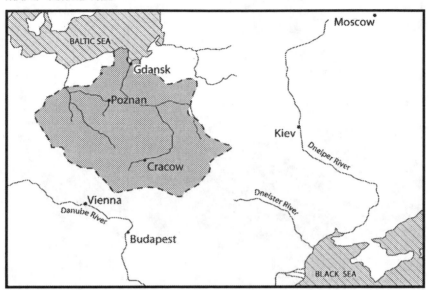

MAP III - Poland 1466

Poland and Lithuania were united under one ruler in 1386.

MAP IV - Poland 1939

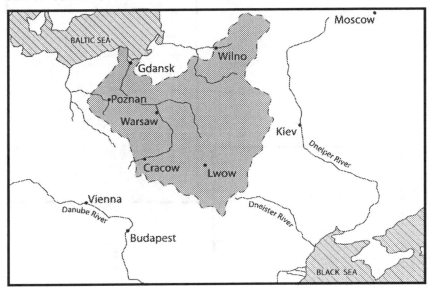

MAP V - Poland 1945

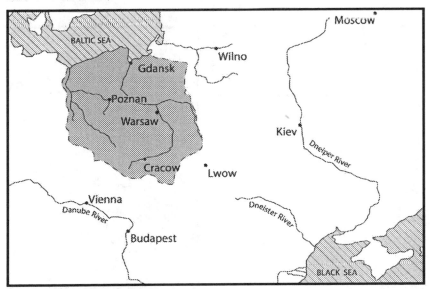

MAP VI - Partitioning Poland

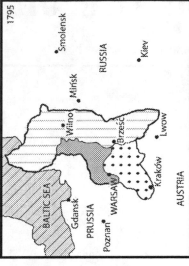

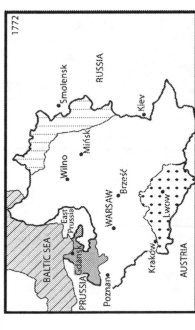

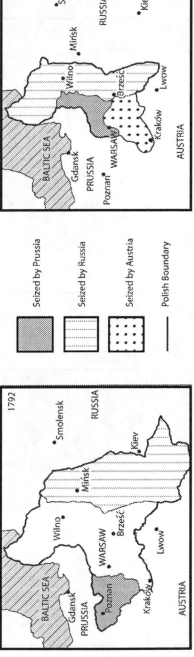

Seized by Prussia

Seized by Russia

Seized by Austria

Polish Boundary

MAP VII - Europe and the Mediterranean, Route of the Treasures 1939-40

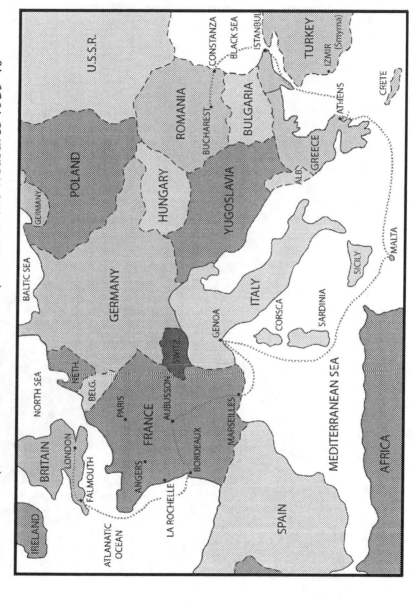

MAP VIII - Eastern North America

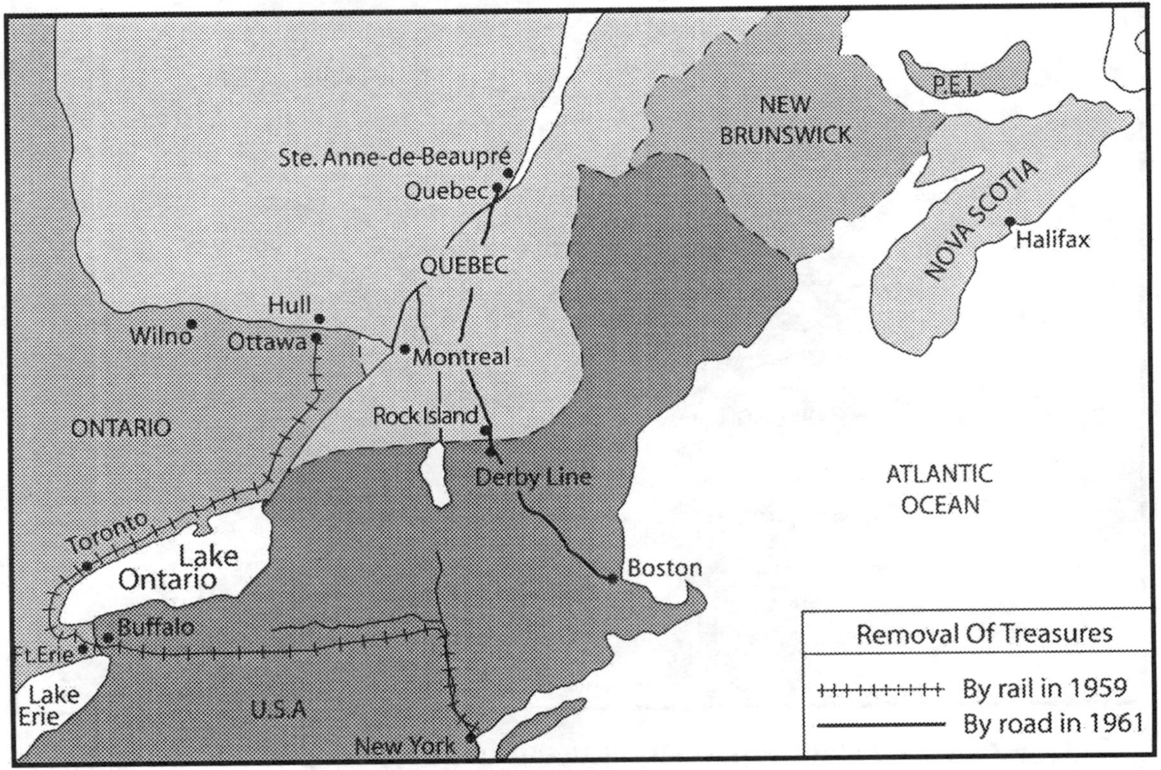

Removal Of Treasures

++++++++ By rail in 1959
———— By road in 1961

P.E.I.

NOVA SCOTIA

Halifax

NEW
BRUNSWICK

ATLANTIC
OCEAN

Ste.Anne-de-Beaupré

Quebec

QUEBEC

Montreal

Rock Island

Derby Line

Boston

Hull

Ottawa

Wilno

Lake
Ontario

ONTARIO

Toronto

Buffalo

Ft.Erie

Lake
Erie

New York

U.S.A

CHAPTER ONE
The Storm Clouds Gather

Concern for the royal treasures of the Wawel Castle, Cracow, mounted during the early months of 1939 as Poland faced the threat of Nazi invasion. Plans for the removal of the treasures to a place of safekeeping were finalized in March. Not all the castle's valuable artifacts could be evacuated to a secure location, but the superintendent of the Wawel Castle was determined to protect the most ancient and valuable historical objects. Twenty special large metal trunks were ordered from a local tinsmith, together with seven long metal cylinders designed to hold the tapestries that graced the walls of the royal apartments and assembly rooms in the castle.[1]

Why the concern about Cracow when Warsaw was the capital of the Republic of Poland? Why were so many valuable national treasures to be found on Wawel Hill in the southern city of Cracow? Actually, Cracow had served as the capital of the Kingdom of Poland almost from its inception, retaining that honour for more than five hundred years. During the Middle Ages and on through the Renaissance, the fortified Wawel Hill on the bank of the Vistula River served as the royal residence and administrative centre of the Polish kingdom. From their base in Cracow in the fifteenth and sixteenth centuries the Jagiellonian kings ruled the largest state in Europe; Poland stretched from the Baltic in the north to the Black Sea in the south, from Poznan in the west to a frontier close to Moscow and the Crimean peninsula in the east.

The Polish Commonwealth of this time was one of the most progressive states in Europe.* The *seym*, or parliament of Poland,

---

*Concerning the use of the term "commonwealth": Poland and Lithuania had been brought together under one king in 1386, when Wládisláw Jagiello, the

17

which had developed first on a regional basis, had became a truly national institution by 1468. Along with parliamentary government came the development of civil liberties for the people of Poland. Under the Commonwealth, no citizen could be imprisoned without a trial; the king could neither raise troops nor levy taxes to pay for an army without the consent of the seym; and freedom of the press was guaranteed. Religious tolerance was another characteristic of the Polish state in the days of the Jagiellonian kings. Jews in large numbers had been welcomed into Poland in the fourteenth century by King Kasimierz the Great and thereafter made up a sizable proportion of the population. Moreover, Poland suffered none of the religious wars between Protestants and Catholics that were to plague the rest of Europe after the Reformation. This freedom to practise any religion without discrimination was finally formally established in the constitution in 1573.[2]

Nor did the Polish Commonwealth neglect intellectual pursuits. The University of Cracow was the second to be founded in central Europe (preceded only by the Charles University in Prague). This university became renowned for its high standard of scholarship, attracting such students as Nicolas Copernicus, who later went on to formulate his heliocentric model of the universe. The first Polish printing press was established in Cracow in 1473, three years before William Caxton set up the first English press in London.[*] During this

---

Grand Duke of Lithuania, was crowned King of Poland, becoming the first king of the famed Jagiellonian dynasty. In 1569 an Act of Union was negotiated in Lublin to establish one *seym*, or parliament, to legislate for the two countries, and one administration with ministers appointed from both nations. At this time the term "commonwealth" was applied to the Polish-Lithuanian state, which formally became "the Most Serene Commonwealth of the Two Nations" (Adam Zurowski, *The Polish Way*, pp. 93–94). This was almost a century before the English Puritans used the term to describe the government they established after the execution of Charles I, and several centuries before the British Commonwealth of the present day.

[*]Some of the political ideas advocated by Polish scholars of the commonwealth were very radical and far ahead of their time. Grycz-Modrewski advocated the emancipation of the peasants, the equality of all before the law, the state's responsibility for the poor, and a system of state education for all.

same time period, Renaissance scholarship was being introduced into Poland thanks to the royal tutors the Jagiellonian kings had recruited from Italy. An Italian architect was also hired by King Sigismund I to remodel his medieval castle into the Renaissance-style royal palace that we see today. His son and heir, Sigismund Augustus, ordered a magnificent set of Flemish tapestries that were specifically designed to fit the walls of the newly renovated royal residence. Such was the society that was thriving in Poland and particularly in Cracow, its capital, in this heyday of the Polish monarchy.[3]

But fortune is fickle — and no less so in the field of politics than in any other aspect of human endeavour. During the seventeenth and eighteenth centuries, the power of the central government in Poland declined disastrously. At the same time, Poland's neighbours — Sweden, Russia, Prussia, Austria — were expanding their strength and their military resources. In 1655–56, Swedish armies swept across Poland in what became known as "the Swedish deluge." Not only did the Swedes march across the length and breadth of Poland, but the invaders also stripped the country of everything of value that could be moved. Wagon trains carried paintings, sculpture, furniture, and entire libraries back to Sweden. Even today, students of early Polish history find more original manuscripts and documents in the Swedish royal library at Upsala than in Poland.[4]

In the eighteenth century it was the turn of Russia, Prussia and Austria. In three stages, or partitions, they divided Poland amongst themselves and the Polish Commonwealth disappeared from the map of Europe. During the full-scale warfare that accompanied the third partition in 1795, Russian troops were the first to occupy Warsaw. The Empress of Russia, Catherine II, ordered her commanding general to secure the fabulous sixteenth-century tapestries commissioned by

---

Wawrzyniec Goslicki argued that kings should govern *under* the law and *through* the law — they should rule for the benefit of the nation, and their subjects had the right to rebel against a sovereign who ruled badly. These books circulated widely throughout western Europe, exciting sufficient displeasure in England to cause first Elizabeth and then James I to ban the publication of English editions in 1598 and 1607, respectively (see Konrad Syrop, *Between the Hammer and the Anvil*, 44–45).

Sigismund Augustus, which at that time decorated the royal residence in Warsaw. They were dispatched to St. Petersburg, where they remained for more than 125 years — the spoils of war.[5] When the Prussians took over the Polish capital from the Russian army, they too were quick to take advantage of the situation. Seizing control of the royal treasury, they gained access to the Polish crown jewels. After removing the precious stones, they melted down crowns, sceptres and royal insignia for the gold they contained. Only a few items, which had been carefully hidden away, were saved.[6]

During the next 123 years the Polish people lived as the subjects of three foreign governments. Subjects they might be, but their spirit remained Polish. Polish art and literature, music and theatre, and indeed the Polish will to resist continued to survive despite all external pressure. A Polish state was finally reconstituted as the First World War drew to a close. This new republic was proclaimed on November 11, 1918, a day still celebrated by Poles — not as Armistice Day or Remembrance Day, but as their National Independence Day (see Maps II–VI).

By 1939 this Polish Republic was once again under threat of attack. This time the danger to Poland's national security came from Adolf Hitler's Third Reich. The Nazi juggernaut had already overrun Austria in the spring of 1938, the Sudeten frontier of Czechoslovakia later that year, and the rest of Czechoslovakia on March 15, 1939. Poland was next on Hitler's "drive to the east," and the Germans did not waste any time before making their intentions clear. An ultimatum was sent to the government of Poland on March 22 demanding the return of Danzig (Gdansk) as well as the corridor of territory that separated East Prussia from the rest of Germany. Intimidating propaganda from German radio stations bombarded the Polish population with raucous demands and threats. At the end of March, Great Britain offered the Poles an unconditional guarantee of their territorial integrity, and in the following month a full military alliance between Britain, France and Poland was signed. The key to the issue of peace or war lay in Moscow, where both the Germans and the West Europeans were wooing the communist leaders of the U.S.S.R. On August 21 news of a non-aggression pact between Nazi Germany and Communist Russia broke upon a startled world. Hitler's hands were freed for an attack upon Poland without the fear of a confrontation with the Soviet Union. German forces began to mass along the Polish frontier, and the demands broadcast by German radio stations redoubled.[7]

In light of what had happened in the past, it is easy to understand the concern of Stanisláw Taszakowski, the superintendent of the Wawel, for the Polish royal treasures that had been entrusted to his care. At the beginning of the crisis, no steps had been taken to remove and pack the royal treasures because it was considered that this activity might spread alarm among the people of Cracow. On August 16, however, the castle was closed to the public and the process of packing the most valuable artifacts began in earnest.[8]

Probably the most important object scheduled for removal was Szczerbiec, the notched sword. This two-handed battle sword was first used in 1320 at the coronation of Wládisláw I, one of the most important medieval Polish kings. Wládisláw, nicknamed "Lokietek" or "Elbow High," may have been short but he did prove to be an able ruler, fighting off an invasion from Bohemia and re-establishing the unity of Poland after a period of disruption and decline.* Thereafter, Szczerbiec was used at the crowning of every Polish king until 1764, when Stanisláw Augustus Poniatowski took the throne. Tradition stated that a king who did not use the notched sword at his coronation would run the risk of endangering the borders of his country, and misfortune did indeed follow Stanisláw Augustus. He not only had to preside over the diminution of Poland's territory through two partitions, but he ultimately had to face the total elimination of his country in 1795. Szczerbiec was seized by the Prussians at this time, along with the rest of the coronation regalia. While everything else was melted down for its gold content, the notched battle sword survived, becoming in the twentieth century a much revered object that linked a newly reconstituted Poland with its historic traditions. And so, on an August day in 1939 Szczerbiec, the iron

---

*Polish kings have been given a strange and colourful array of names. In addition to Wládisláw I Lokietek, we have Bolesláw III Krzywousty (Bolesláw the Wry Mouth) as well as Augustus II Mocny (Augustus the Strong), so named either because he could break a horseshoe with one hand or because of his sexual prowess in begetting more than 300 offspring. (See Adam Zurowski, *The Polish Way*, 18, 208.)

coronation sword with its bejewelled and marvellously engraved hilt, was carefully packed away.[9]

The few other symbols of royal authority that had survived over the years received similar careful attention. These included a sword, scabbard and belt presented to King Jan Sobieski by Pope Innocent XI in gratitude for the role Sobieski had played in raising the Turkish siege of Vienna in 1683. The Pope had also presented Sobieski with a purple velvet hat decorated with a dove, the symbol of the Holy Ghost, embroidered in pearls. A cloak of black velvet, embellished with silver and gold embroidery and belonging to the Order of the Holy Spirit, was also presented to Sobieski by King Louis XIV of France to honour the military victory at Vienna. A Turkish sword captured at Vienna, as well as a number of jewelled batons — the symbols of authority belonging to Polish *hetmen*, or generals — were also stored away to complement the symbol of Polish royal authority.[10]

Among the most valuable items of the Wawel national treasure was the collection of Flemish tapestries, or arrases, that King Sigismund Augustus had commissioned from workshops in the vicinity of Brussels in the sixteenth century. The tapestries were first displayed in 1553 on the occasion of the marriage of Sigismund Augustus to Catherine of Hapsburg, who was, incidentally, the Jagiellonian monarch's third wife. In his last will, King Sigismund bequeathed all of these tapestries to his sisters, provided that they become state property after the sisters died.

Some of these Polish state tapestries were surprisingly large, stretching as much as five metres across. Woven of silk, as well as gold and silver thread, they were masterpieces of the art of needlework. Many of the larger pieces depicted important religious scenes such as the story of Creation or that of the flood and the rescue of Noah and his family. To do justice to any particular theme might require several tapestries — for instance the four Creation arrases showed God creating Adam, Adam and Eve in the Garden of Eden, their banishment, and the subsequent hard labour required to produce the fruits of the earth. These particular events were depicted with a beauty and realism that astonished and moved viewers greatly, so much so that the authorities decided that the moral sensibilities of the public had to be protected by attaching specially woven fig leaves to the naked bodies of Adam and Eve in the Creation tapestries. In addition to the biblical scenes there were many smaller tapestries representing animals against scenic backgrounds as well as others with grotesque or floral motifs. These smaller pieces were designed to fit narrow wall spaces or to be placed above a panel of windows in the Wawel palace.[11]

The magnificent collection of over 300 tapestries that Sigismund Augustus had finally assembled did not fare well over the centuries. During the seventeenth century, one of the more impecunious Polish kings found himself extremely short of money and pawned 157 of the Wawel tapestries to a Gdansk merchant. They were eventually redeemed in the eighteenth century, only to fall prey to the Russians at the time of the Polish partitions, when Empress Catherine had them transported to St. Petersburg. Some of the arrases went to adorn the Winter Palace there, while others were allotted to various museums and palaces throughout Russia. Those that were too large to fit the rooms to which they were assigned were cut down to size. Other tapestries were mutilated where doorways or fireplaces needed to be exposed, or they were cut to provide upholstery coverings for chairs or sofas. After the czarist regime was overthrown in the Russian Revolution, the tapestries were returned to Poland by the Soviet government. This shipment comprised less than half of King Sigismund's original collection. It was these 136 very special arrases, housed in their original home in the Wawel Castle, that were now taken down and stowed away in seven long metal tubes that had been constructed for that purpose earlier in the year.[12]

Many other precious objects required great care. There were thirteen gold mugs and cups, a seventeenth-century coffee service in gold, as well as two ornamental clocks dating from the same time period. Three suits of medieval armour, together with a sixteenth-century eastern European helmet, engraved and gold-plated, had to be packed, along with fifteen cavalry saddles from the seventeenth century, jewelled and ornamented with gold and silver.[13]

Once the packing of the twenty metal trunks and the seven tubes holding the Wawel tapestries had been completed, Superintendent Taszakowski called an emergency meeting of his staff to discuss the evacuation of the Polish national treasures from the Wawel in the event of war. The Polish army would provide the necessary transportation to move the valuable artifacts east to Jaroslàv. There they would remain in safekeeping until the battle lines between the Polish and German troops had been stabilized with the promised support of British and French forces.[14] With plans so carefully laid, it was expected that all should go well.

The royal castle on Wawel Hill in Cracow.

The royal palace inside the castle on Wawel Hill.

Goblet with effigy of King Jan Sobieski III, who was famous for breaking the Turkish siege of Vienna in 1683.

One of the large Flemish tapestries woven for King Sigimund Augustus (1548–1572), depicting Noah and his family building the ark.

Another Flemish tapestry: Noah and his wife gather the animals, two by two, into the ark.

CHAPTER TWO
Escape

On Friday, August 30, 1939, Jozef Polkowski, one of the senior staff members at the Wawel Castle, was summoned to attend a very important meeting of the Cracow civil defence commanders. One year before, Polkowski had been sent on an aviation defence course so that he could take charge of such matters at the castle. Now the time to undertake serious air defence measures had arrived. The district commanders were informed that a nationwide anti-aircraft emergency had been declared at 1:00 that afternoon and that the national civil defence plan was to be implemented immediately. The consensus at the meeting was that war could be expected at any moment.[15]

Born at Plock, near Warsaw, in 1888, Jozef Krzywda Polkowski had not had an easy childhood. His mother had died when he was four years old, leaving his grandmother to take care of the family. At the age of fourteen he had lost his father, and soon thereafter he moved to Smolensk to stay with a friend of the family. These people were very good to him, and two years later they sent him to Moscow to further his education. Polkowski was accepted into the Moscow Academy of Architecture, Painting and Sculpture where he obtained a degree in architecture in 1911. During the First World War he served in the Russian Imperial Army and later in the Polish army that was engaged in repelling the Russian invasion of 1920. Four years later Jozef Polkowski began his fifteen-year association with the Wawel Castle in Cracow.[19] The royal castle had been declared a national museum in 1918, just as Poland regained its independence. Extensive restoration work was necessary, however, since the Austrians had used the castle as a barracks during the years prior to the war when they had ruled southern Poland. And so Polkowski was hired as an architect to work on what must have been a very exciting restoration project. In order to refurbish the castle as a museum, a program had been organized to recover the art treasures that had formerly graced the royal palace. In addition to his other duties Polkowski had been made an assistant curator of this state art collection.[17]

By 1939 Polkowski was fifty-one years old, married and a respected member of the Wawel Castle staff. A tall, well-built, clean-shaven man, he dressed meticulously. Although soft spoken, he had a strong personality and a set of convictions, both religious and patriotic, that could not be easily overridden. His fine features and aristocratic bearing marked him as a man to be noticed, even in a crowd.[18]

When Polkowski, as civil defence coordinator for the Wawel Castle, returned from the August 30 Cracow conference, Superintendent Taszakowski refused to implement his defence proposals, and a heated argument ensued. The commander of the castle, Dr. Adolf Szyszko Bohusz — the final authority over the entire Wawel Castle complex — overheard the altercation and intervened in support of Polkowski. Taszakowski was told to follow the instructions of the Wawel's defence commander. The famed tapestries of King Sigismund Augustus were to be taken down from the walls of the castle immediately and packed away in the long metal tubes that had been constructed to protect them in transit.

Saturday evening found Polkowski at his command post in the Wawel Castle with all his air defence stations on a state of high alert. Finally, at 3:30 a.m. he turned over his command to his subordinate and retired to catch some sleep. An hour later he was awakened by someone pounding at his door to announce that German troops had crossed the frontier. Polkowski ran out of his apartment to sound the alarm. Quickly, people began to gather in the bomb shelter that had been prepared in the southwest corner of the castle. Within minutes the first bombers flew over the city and Cracow's airfield was under attack. The war was on!

It was now Sunday, September 1, and the staff at the Wawel spent a confusing, anxious day trying to determine what was happening in the country at large. It would prove to be a very long day of watching and waiting. Later, in the evening, they learned that the airport had been bombed a second time. The next day proved no better, with air raids continuing throughout the morning. Then, around six o'clock in the evening, nine Heinkels approached from the southwest, following along the Vistula River right past Wawel Hill. The formation was fired upon by the guns positioned in front of the Wawel, whereupon the planes moved on to attack the Cracow radio station. This they completely destroyed, leaving the city virtually cut off from news about what was happening in the rest of Poland. Around 9:00 p.m. Polkowski was able to get in touch with the military radio station, from which he learned that the war was going badly. The Polish army was retreating on every front. In their area, the Germans were approaching Cracow along the Vistula valley from the west, while other enemy troops were advancing from the south in an attempt to surround the city. Obviously, something needed to be done quickly if the Wawel treasures were to be saved.

Polkowski waited impatiently for the morning to come in order to consult with Stanisláw Taszakowski, the castle administrator. At 5:00 a.m. on Tuesday, September 3, he awakened Taszakowski and explained the situation. The administrator agreed that conditions were desperate. The collections had to be removed that very day. Unfortunately, the army trucks that had been promised for the evacuation of the Wawel Castle were simply not available because the Polish army needed every vehicle it could commandeer for military purposes. Communication with Warsaw proved impossible because the telephone lines had been cut. The two men, however, did get through to the local township (*voivode*) office, only to be told that the mayor had left the evening before and that the entire office was, at that moment, being evacuated. The railway office reported that the Luftwaffe had blown up key sections of track and destroyed so many bridges that nothing was moving by rail. The city police were approached for help but their trucks had all been taken by the army. The carefully laid plans for the evacuation of the royal treasure had gone very much awry and some alternative would have to be improvised.

If the metal trunks and containers could not be moved by land, there remained only the Vistula River, a busy commercial highway during normal times. Two very abnormal days had passed, however, and already most of the river barges had been commandeered by groups of refugees anxious to make their way downstream out of the path of the Wehrmacht. The director of river transport, one of the few government officials who still remained at his post, did promise to look for some form of water transportation for them. The Wawel staff was therefore ordered to move the packed cases to the Grand Lobby on the ground floor of the castle ready for shipment. At this point Taszakowski finally succeeded in contacting the Warsaw government. He was instructed to evacuate the collections immediately, along with the Wawel staff and their families and the sacristans from the cathedral, to a destination of his own choosing.

Around eleven o'clock in the morning Dr. Szyszko Bohusz, the Commandant of the Castle, arrived. Once he was made aware of the desperate nature of the situation, Bohusz endorsed the plan for the immediate evacuation of the castle. Taszakowski and Szysko Bohusz then asked Polkowski to take command of transportation during the trip. Polkowski agreed, assuring them that he was, in any case, obliged to fulfill this duty by the mobilization plan. He also hoped that that this would give him a chance to contact his wife, who was at that time staying with her brother at Leczyca, west of Warsaw. Bohusz then sent for Dr. Stanisláw Swierz Zaleski, the chief curator of the Wawel collection, to acquaint him with the most recent plans.[19]

Dr. Zaleski, born in 1886, had obtained his Ph.D. in art history from the Jagiellonian University in Cracow. Besides working as an appraiser of paintings, he had been appointed curator of the state art collection at the Wawel Castle in 1929, becoming chief curator ten years later. Zaleski was a dark-haired, medium-sized man with a bland face and a moustache, rather negligent in his manner of dress. He was a sensitive and capable painter of considerable talent, which probably explains his appointment as art curator at the Wawel. In dealing with other people he tended to be timid and pliant and yet, underneath all of this, he was a very self-centred person.[20]

When Zaleski appeared as a result of Bohusz's summons, Taszakowski informed him about the decision to evacuate the treasures from the Wawel and told him to travel with the collection in order to look after the art treasures when they reached their destination. According to Polkowski, Zaleski refused categorically. He said that family matters came first at a time like this and that he had to join his wife in Zakopane. He also argued that the Germans, being a highly cultured nation, would not stoop so low as to seize Poland's national treasures. When Taszakowski threatened to remove him from his position as chief curator of the collection, Zaleski capitulated and consented to go. All three officials then agreed that they would head eastward about 120 kilometres to the city of Jarosław as soon as possible.

Around five o'clock in the evening the director of river traffic called. He had a coal barge which had just discharged its cargo at the waterfront, and this would be placed at the disposal of the Wawel officials. The police promised to cooperate by delivering the metal cases to the barge. Around 6:00 p.m. a policeman did indeed arrive with a small tractor pulling a wagon that was normally used for transporting manure. The Wawel caretakers immediately started loading the trunks onto the wagon for delivery to the dock, an operation that required several trips. At the last minute a number of used carpets from the castle were added to the collection on the grounds that they might prove useful. Polkowski and Zaleski left the Wawel with the last transport to the dockside around 8:30 p.m. As they passed the cathedral, the parish priest and his curate were waiting to bless them and wish them a safe return.

When Polkowski and Zaleski arrived at the waterfront, they saw the eighty-two evacuees — men, women and children — gathered around the chests from the castle. Nearby was a deserted barge tied up on the river's edge. They ordered the policeman who had driven their tractor to search for the bargeman and return with him as quickly as possible. Then they set the Wawel people to work loading the chests onto the barge. Because the chests and the long tubes for the tapestries were made of shiny, new metal, they gleamed in the dark, reflecting any light in the area. Here the carpets from the Wawel immediately proved useful. They were unrolled and draped over the metal chests to render them relatively inconspicuous. By the time all this had been completed, the policeman had found the barge owner and his helper in a dockside café. The bargeman at first refused to move. He and his assistant had just completed a two-day voyage with next to no sleep and they were in no mood to set out again. The story goes, however, that once he learned what cargo they were being asked to transport, the bargeman said to his helper, "Antoni, we will sleep when we are dead, but we cannot now leave our treasures to the Krauts." With these words the two boatmen moved off to man their barge.

The barge set off at precisely nine o'clock. The national treasures from the castle were stored amidships; the Wawel staff and their families could be found huddled together in the stern with their baggage; and the bargeman, Zaleski and Polkowski took their places forward. The bargeman, Franciszek Misia, soon earned Polkowski's respect by his expert handling of the vessel as well as by his innate common sense. Asked about their options, Misia replied that they would run with the current because there was no other alternative. Since the water levels were extremely low, however, they would not make much progress without a tugboat — a resource that was just not available. Setting aside this problem for another day, the Wawel personnel soon settled down to sleep, exhausted by their three-day vigil at the castle. This left Misia and his helper, fifteen-year-old Antoni Novak, to guide the barge throughout the night, maintaining their position in the swiftest flow of water by careful poling.[21] (For their escape route, see Map I.)

CHAPTER THREE
Tough Decisions

Just before dawn when Jozef Polkowski awoke, the bargeman proposed stopping nearby to buy some milk and eggs from a farmer he knew. This would give everyone a chance to relieve themselves and walk around for a few minutes. When the barge reached shore, everybody raced for the bushes and then, as soon as the farm supplies had been obtained, they set off again. The adult males were divided into groups of four and set to work poling the barge because the river had broadened out and the current had become very sluggish. During this time, formations of German planes could be seen. Fearing that the barge might attract their attention, the Wawel curators decided to pull into shore and hide the barge among the reeds. The men also cut reeds to camouflage the vessel so that it looked like a small island. This break gave the boatmen the opportunity for an hour's sleep before setting out again. When night fell, they continued to press on, travel under the cover of darkness being considered safer than running the river in broad daylight.

The next morning — Thursday, September 5 — the boatmen tied up their barge and Polkowski and several of the caretakers went into town to buy supplies and to get some information about the state of affairs throughout the country. About the progress of the war there were only conflicting rumours, but the men did manage to purchase bread, butter, eggs, and even a few hens. They set out again and the women prepared a meal, using the camp stoves and cooking pots they had brought from the castle. This was the first proper meal they had managed to put together since leaving the Wawel Castle.

That afternoon they ran into much traffic on the Vistula River. As one of the motor boats went past, someone on the barge recognized the director of river traffic from Cracow. The Wawel refugees called to him frantically, but to no avail. His motorboat, the *Pawel*, put into shore a short distance downstream, however, and Polkowski ordered the boatman to follow him. Unfortunately, the barge had to stop on the opposite bank because of the shallow water. Swierz Zaleski and Franciszek Misia waded through water up to their waists to the motor vessel in order to talk to the director of water transport. Recognizing two members of the Wawel expedition and mindful of the valuable cargo they were transporting, the director agreed to attach a tow line and assist them along their way. At 6:00 p.m. the *Pawel* was ready to depart with the barge from the Wawel in tow.[22] Night on the river had already proved cold and damp and Polkowski was worried about the well-being of the women and children. He produced a bottle of vodka and measured out a small quantity to each of them to warm their spirits.[23] Then, sometime after ten o'clock, they had to stop because of thick fog on the river.

On Saturday, September 7, they reached Sandomierz — where, according to their original plan, they were supposed to disembark and take the train to Jarosláw. This proved impossible because the city was in chaos. The city council office stood wide open, papers and cases abandoned, with not a soul in sight. The post office and a high-security prison were also open and deserted and there was not a policeman to be seen in the city. The men from the barge did see soldiers on the road, cutting down trees to build anti-tank barriers. They were told that the German army was very close. Indeed the Sandomierz train station had already been destroyed by bombs and there was no possibility of travelling by rail. An air raid occurred while the Wawel staff reconnoitred the city; two more followed before they returned to the barge. Under the circumstances there was nothing they could do but continue to travel the river. The air raids lasted all day — the men counted nineteen in all — with formations of twelve or more bombers in each flight. Poland was taking a terrible beating.

At dusk, the barge departed, overtaking the *Pawel* at the outskirts of the city. Because the Polish forces had now retreated to the east side of the Vistula, the two vessels kept close to the right-hand bank, proceeding as quietly as possible. Once again, as on the previous night, thick fog caused them to put into shore early. The next day they continued on at dawn, through air raids that were as bad as ever. Often the explosions were quite close, so it was no surprise that, by this time, they were passing many sunken boats and barges stranded in the Vistula. Polkowski asked the captain of the *Pawel* to proceed as quickly as possible to get out of the danger zone. Later, when it was already quite dark, the two vessels made their way under a bridge. Continuing on for about a kilometre, they heard heavy gunfire behind them, followed by a violent explosion whose shock waves rocked the barge. After a while, when they had been stopped by the Polish army, they learned that the massive explosion had been caused by a German tank that had been blown up while pushing a trailer loaded with explosives intended to demolish the local bridge. Fortunately, the Polish army patrol allowed the group of Wawel refugees to continue downstream.

On September 9 the little convoy reached Kasimierz. At this point it seemed imperative to get off the Vistula River. German tanks had been spotted on the west bank of the river and it was impossible to continue further down a waterway that had become the battle line between two armies. Moreover, it was reported that the bridges across the Vistula downstream from Kasimierz were under constant bombardment from German artillery and aircraft. Polkowski and Dr. Zaleski proceeded into town to look for help. The people's militia directed them to the local postmaster, Leopold Pisz, who might be able to make the necessary telephone connections for them to secure further advice. A few months earlier this gentleman had visited Cracow, where he had been most impressed by the Polish national treasures displayed at the Wawel Castle. Although he had received orders to evacuate his post that day, he agreed to remain on duty and try to repair the telephone lines in order to get help for the Wawel evacuees. He told the two men to return in the evening to find out what he had accomplished.

Returning to the barge, Polkowski and Zaleski were faced with some difficult decisions. They knew that they could not hope to find transportation over land for eighty-two people. Since their prime responsibility was to safeguard the national treasures, some other alternative would have to be found for the rest of the Wawel staff. It was decided that the sacristans from the cathedral should leave in rented wagons for Lublin, where they could get help from the bishop's entourage. The caretakers and their families from the castle would also head for Lublin by a different route. Only Polkowski, Zaleski and four of the caretakers would continue to travel with the Polish treasures.

After the departure of their comrades, the barge owner received orders to disembark the cases and trunks at the winter port. While Dr. Zaleski returned to the post office to discover what sort of help they could expect, Polkowski and the four caretakers who remained with him unloaded the barge. Bidding farewell to the two boatmen who had laboured so hard for them for almost a week was one of the more difficult moments on this long saga of escape.[24] It was largely due to the skill of these two men that the Wawel treasures had made it this far. In his memoirs written many years later, Polkowski attributed their success in rescuing the Polish art treasures to Misia and Antoni Nowak.[25] After saying their goodbyes and parting from the boatmen, the caretakers from the Wawel expedition prepared to spend the night by their cases, which had been placed under the trees beside the road. Around midnight Zaleski returned from the post office to report that they could expect some kind of transportation the following day.

Around eight o'clock the next morning, twelve peasant wagons arrived under the command of an army corporal. This was the transportation dispatched to start the Wawel refugees on their way. Unfortunately, when they reached the next village after an hour's ride, the drivers stopped at the village office and refused to go any further. They said that they had fulfilled their instructions, and the corporal confirmed that such was indeed the case. Polkowski refused to remove the cases from the wagons and persuaded the corporal to seek further instructions from his commander. The answer came back in about an hour. They were to unload the peasants' wagons and confiscate others to meet their requirements. This was a mockery since all the other wagons in the village had already been commandeered by the army. With the help of the village reeve, Polkowski convinced the peasants to transport them at least to the next village. Dr. Zaleski took his place in the first wagon and Polkowski got into the last and they departed again. They had barely entered the next village when the reeve of this community started screaming at the peasants and ordered them to move on, threatening them with a shotgun. Without a word of protest the peasants started their horses and proceeded onward, much to the delight of the Wawel curators.

About midafternoon a formation of German airplanes appeared, from which one plane detached itself in order to investigate the wagon train. The drivers stopped the horses and everyone scattered into the potato fields seeking shelter. The airplane flew very low over the wagons, did no damage and departed, much to everyone's relief. A little further along, however, another altercation with the peasants occurred. One of them drove the wheel of his wagon into some soft sand, which brought the vehicle to a halt. He declared that he would go no further, and neither would his neighbours. Being removed from their own village and their families at this time of mass confusion and distress was proving too much for the peasants to endure. By threatening them with a court martial for sabotage in wartime, however, Polkowski persuaded them to continue. After securing a promise of wagons for the next day from the magistrate in the next village, Polkowski unloaded the cases in a forest on the edge of town and let the peasants go, giving them a generous payment for the use of their vehicles throughout the day.

At daybreak on September 11, Zaleski set out for the nearest town in hopes of getting a telephone connection with the Lublin authorities. Returning in the afternoon, Zaleski reported that the postmaster from Kasimierz had already got through to Lublin, reporting the location of the national treasures and the direction in which they were travelling. That evening the local village reeve delivered thirteen wagons as promised and the convoy set out again. They reached the next village in the dead of night and stopped at the last farm yard, where the farmer allowed them to unload the collection in his barn.

Next morning, their first task was to secure further transportation. The local authorities could hardly have been more obstructive. The village administrator sent them to the commander of the police station, who examined their papers and then insisted on inspecting the contents of their cases. He eventually promised to send them transportation by midafternoon and then departed. At 4:00 p.m. one wagon arrived, pulled by a lame horse — the promised transportation, presumably. It would not take them far. Two hours later a special envoy arrived from

Lublin to instruct them to be at the village of Tomaszowice by 4:00 a.m., where they would find motorized transport waiting to take them on their way. Since they still had no wagons, they had to approach the police commander once more. When he proved as uncooperative as ever, Polkowski threatened dire consequences if he obstructed military orders. This conversation motivated the commander to take action, and by midnight the wagons arrived equipped with decent horses. The men quickly loaded the collection and started off. During the night they overtook the Wawel caretakers and their wives and children — the entire party that had set out for Lublin from Kasimierz three days before — in an unexpected and joyous reunion.[26]

It was early morning on September 13 when the Wawel party reached Tomaszowice. Three Warsaw buses and a truck awaited them, manned by Warsaw tram drivers and escorted by military personnel under the command of a retired army colonel. These buses were supposed to transport ammunition from that area to Warsaw, but lines of communication had broken down and they were ordered to evacuate the Wawel treasures instead. As soon as they began stowing away the luggage, the men discovered that the long, tubular cases that held the tapestries would not fit through the doors of the buses — they would have to be loaded onto the truck. The women and children were then placed in the one bus that still had seats, while the men rode with the rest of the collection in the other two buses. By 8:00 a.m. they reached Lublin, a city that by this time was serving as the temporary seat of the Polish government. Lublin had been bombed frequently, the last raid having occurred only the night before. In the business district rows of buildings had been destroyed, the remaining houses were still smouldering and bodies were lying in the streets unattended. There was nothing for the Wawel refugees to do but continue their journey.

Bypassing Zamosc, the next major centre, they headed east toward the Bug River. About 10 kilometres along the route the bus in which the women and children were travelling broke down with a flat tire. The colonel, arriving in his Buick, told the rest of the convoy to continue on their way. He assured them that he would take care of the tire so that the rest of the party could catch them up before long. They did not see the colonel again until 9:00 p.m., when it became clear that he had done nothing to rescue the women and children on the stranded bus. Apparently, from his exalted viewpoint, they could be left to fend for themselves. Not long after this encounter with the colonel, word arrived from headquarters that all military divisions, including the Wawel contingent, were to depart for Luck, about 100 kilometres further east. At this moment there was nothing that the Wawel party could do for their companions on the stranded bus. They did learn later that most of them made their way on foot to Zamosc, where they were helped by the local bishop to return to Cracow. At this point, however, the Wawel curators had to depart immediately for Luck with their shipment of national treasures. Their progress on the road was slow and very hazardous since they had to drive without lights in a long string of traffic. They finally reached their destination, completely exhausted, at 4:00 a.m.

On this date, September 14, the Polish government could be found at Luck. Before the day was out, however, the government officials were on the road again. That same day the Wawel personnel also witnessed the departure of a large shipment of Polish bullion which was carried in two covered trucks, escorted by cars of steel-helmeted policemen armed with machine guns. The colonel left the Wawel staff at Luck, entrusting them and their valuable consignment of national treasures to a major and a second lieutenant of the Polish armed forces. It took the entire day for their new escorts to get ready for the road, so their departure did not take place until evening. They travelled south along Poland's eastern border for the next few days without any major mishap.[27]

Then, on September 17, without warning, Russian troops invaded Poland from the east and it became absolutely clear what lay behind the Russo-German non-aggression pact signed less than a month before. Once again Poland was to be wiped off the map, divided between her two large neighbours to the east and west. This was the common ground that brought together the leaders of two conflicting ideologies in a cynical partnership of greed. For the Wawel refugees, with hostile forces now approaching from both east and west, there was not a moment to lose. Crossing the Polish border into Romania had become imperative. There was no other safe haven for the Polish national treasures entrusted to the care of the Wawel curators.

The men drove frantically all that day to reach the town of Kuty, which was situated on a small river that marked the vital Polish-Romanian border. As they approached Kuty late on that night of September 17, the curators found the roads completely jammed with motor traffic. It was only with great difficulty that they nosed their rather large vehicles into the line of cars entering the town. All these cars were heading for the main street that led to the bridge that crossed the river and into Romania. Eventually, when the cars in front of them began to move, they followed the flow of traffic.[28]

Polkowski tells the story of the river crossing quite dramatically:

> Around 2:30 a.m. we entered the border bridge, brightly lit on its Romanian half. There was a border sign with a White Eagle in the middle of the bridge. We took off our hats while passing it, and one of the drivers said: "Gentlemen, look carefully at this symbol of Poland, for it is possible that not many of us will see it again in our lives."[29]

CHAPTER FOUR
Further Voyaging

Having successfully crossed the bridge into Romania, the Polish refugees stopped in the adjacent border settlement to reconnoitre. Some Jewish people in that small village came out into the streets, bringing coffee and milk for the children who were travelling with the adults. When the curators contacted the Polish embassy in Bucharest, they were told to proceed to the capital city, a journey across Romania that took them several more days.[30]

Arriving in Bucharest, they found the Polish embassy in turmoil. The courtyard, and the entire street in front of the embassy, were clogged with the cars of Polish government officials and other refugees. The custodians of the Wawel treasures, Jozef Polkowski and Dr. Stanisláw Swierz Zaleski, had to park their motley vehicles some distance away and walk to the embassy to consult with the Polish authorities about the disposal of their valuable cargo. Unfortunately, the ambassador was absent.[31] Due to the many refugees who were overrunning the embassy, luggage and all, the officials in charge declared that they could only provide accommodation for three of the containers that had been brought from the Wawel Castle.[32] The rest of the collection was to be turned over to King Carol of Romania so that it could be stored in the vaults of the royal palace. The thought of relinquishing to a foreign ruler the Polish treasures that they had rescued with such difficulty from their war-ravaged country appalled Jozef Polkowski. He was extremely reluctant to accede to this request.

In the street outside the embassy the two men met Count Andrew Potocki, who had arrived in Bucharest several days earlier. The count agreed with Polkowski's assessment of the situation. Potocki suggested that he would approach the British consul general, Frank Severy, who had served some years before in a consular position in Poland and was a personal friend of his. Within an hour the count returned to say that everything had been arranged satisfactorily. Severy was able to empty the huge garage at the British embassy so that they could store the rest of their precious belongings there. Once the cases had been stored away, the garage was locked with a padlock whose key was turned over to Jozef Polkowski. The curators could then breathe more easily.[33]

Unfortunately for the Poles, Adolf Hitler's German government had the same access to the Romanian capital as any other country. The curators feared that the Germans would exert pressure on the Romanian government to retrieve for them the Polish art treasures from the Wawel Castle, which special envoys had already carefully enumerated before the outbreak of hostilities.[34] Their fears were not without foundation. On November 4, after a conference with Hitler, Hans Franck recorded his plans to make the Wawel Castle in Cracow the headquarters from which he would rule that part of Poland known as the General Government, that had not been directly annexed to Germany. Franck planned to seize all the valuable Polish treasures he could unearth — national artifacts as well as those in private collections and belonging to the church — and assemble them to adorn his headquarters in the ancient royal castle on Wawel Hill. As part of this program the German ambassador in Bucharest mounted an operation to have the city police seize the cases that had been removed from Poland in September in order that they might be returned to the Wawel Castle. Many Romanians, however, sympathized with the Poles in the face of the dismemberment of their country. Motivated by such views, the commander of the Romanian army placed troops to guard both the Polish and British embassies. When the city police arrived at the Polish embassy to carry out the wishes of their German friends, they found the Romanian army in place. The police had no option but to give up their plans and retreat.[35]

It now seemed imperative to move the Polish national treasures out of Romania to a place of greater safety. Several alternative locations were being discussed at the Polish embassy. Some Polish officials still argued in favour of turning the collection over to King Carol, but the king's increasingly pro-German attitude, along with fears concerning his own designs upon the treasures, rendered this alternative unattractive for most of the Poles. Another proposal was to approach the Vatican to see if it would offer a safe refuge. When the papal nuncio in Bucharest conveyed this request to his superiors in Rome, the answer from the Vatican was not encouraging. Since most of the treasures under discussion were secular rather than religious in nature, the Holy See was not prepared to accept responsibility for the collection.

By this time the Polish government-in-exile had moved on from Romania to establish its headquarters in France, Poland's traditional ally in western Europe. Orders came from the government that the custodians of the national treasure should also move their priceless articles to France as quickly as possible.[36] The government-in-exile placed Dr. Zaleski in charge of the collection, with Polkowski as his assistant, and also appointed two of the workmen from the Wawel to help with the move.[37] A French moving company agreed to look after the travel arrangements, and on November 18 Polkowski and Zaleski supervised the removal of the treasures to the Bucharest station for shipment to Constanza, a port on the Black Sea. Four days later they set sail on a Romanian freighter, the *Ardeal*, which was carrying a cargo of barley to Genoa. From there they were to proceed to Marseilles to unload the Wawel collection, along with ninety soldiers who were heading for France to join the Polish army being reconstituted there to continue the fight against the Third Reich.[38] (See Map VII — Europe and the Mediterranean Sea.)

At the start of her voyage through the Black Sea on November 22 the *Ardeal* was beset by a violent storm.[39] The next day, however, things had calmed down and they sailed through the narrow Turkish waterways — the Bosporus and the Dardanelles straits — past Constantinople (Istanbul) and out into the Aegean Sea in beautiful weather. As they sailed past numerous Aegean islands, a naval vessel belonging to the British Mediterranean Fleet appeared from behind one of them and stopped the *Ardeal*. Tension mounted as the British checked the captain's papers, but fortunately all was in order and the ship was allowed to proceed.[40]

Two days later they reached Piraeus, the port of the city of Athens. A functionary from the Polish legation arrived promptly with an offer to take them into Athens by car. The Polish envoy, Dr. W.S. Gunther, greeted them very cordially at the legation and suggested that they visit the Acropolis and the Parthenon and return for lunch. There was not a single tourist on the sacred hill, and Polkowski and Zaleski took advantage of the opportunity to take some photographs of the site that was the heart of ancient Athens. The weather was drizzly for the most part, but at one moment the clouds parted and the light showed the local olive groves gleaming in superb, rain-refreshed greenery. The two men had to hurry to complete their sightseeing expedition in time for their one o'clock luncheon engagement at the legation. Dr. Gunther, being something of a gourmet, served them superb fish accompanied by some excellent Greek wine. Strengthened in body and in spirit, they returned to the city to visit the Museum of Antiquities, a treasure trove of ancient sculpture and artifacts to which they could scarcely do justice in the short time before they were due back on the *Ardeal*.[41]

At five o'clock, when they reported back to the ship, the Poles were told that they would not leave till late in the evening. They therefore decided to set out to visit the city again. In the harbour area they entered a liquor store whose Greek owner, as it turned out, knew very little of any language but his own. He asked in broken Russian where they came from. Finding out that they were Poles, he exclaimed "*German pfuj! Polska hurra!*" and proceeded to close his store and ask what he could do for them. Polkowski and Zaleski wanted some brandy, so the storekeeper opened four different types of brandy for them to taste. During the tasting the five companions managed to empty all four bottles — all that to buy one for the journey! The Poles staggered back to the ship and threw themselves on their beds with kind memories of Greek friendship and hospitality. All in all, the day had proved one of the better ones along their journey.[42]

From Athens the *Ardeal* crossed the Aegean Sea to Smyrna (Izmir), a Turkish city located about halfway down the coast of Asia Minor, where they spent the entire day on November 27. Two days out of Smyrna their ship was again stopped by the British naval vessel they had dealt with five days before. This time the attitude of the British had changed: a Royal Navy officer and four British sailors were stationed aboard the *Ardeal* to take the ship into the British naval base at Malta.[43] Apparently there was grave concern over the shipment of grain destined for Genoa. Italy, not having issued a declaration of war, was still a neutral nation in November 1939. Mussolini had, however, joined Hitler to form the Rome-Berlin Axis in 1936 and the British feared that grain unloaded at Genoa might well be destined for Nazi Germany.

The Polish treasures and their curators arrived in the port of Valetta, Malta, on December 1. There the *Ardeal* was taken into custody and carefully searched. Not knowing how long they might be detained in Malta, Polkowski and Zaleski remembered that they had entertained the Chevalier Scikluna, the director of the archives of the Knights of Malta, at the Wawel Castle during an international meeting of art historians two years earlier. They dispatched a Maltese gendarme with a letter asking for his help. The next day the Polish honorary consul, a Mr. England, arrived on board with apologies from the chevalier because he could not see them immediately.[44] In the meantime the consul, armed with special landing passes, offered to show them Malta. They found that the island possessed many interesting prehistoric objects, including some very ancient cave paintings. These Maltese caves were used to store food and grain, and they could also serve as air raid shelters in case of an attack on the island. Mr. England proved very kind and provided Polkowski, Zaleski and the large contingent of Polish soldiers with passes to visit the city. The Poles were invited to an opera performance at which the governor of Malta, General Sir Charles Bonham Carter, appealed to the audience to take up a collection for the ninety soldier refugees.[45] Nearly $2,000 was raised to serve as pocket money for the men during their stay on the island.[46]

The honorary consul, Mr. England, and Chevalier Scikluna were finally able to persuade General Bonham Carter that to allow the ninety Polish fighting men to continue on their way to France was more important than any concerns about the ultimate destination of a shipment of barley. The *Ardeal*, which was allowed to depart for Genoa on December 18, arrived on Christmas Day — the Poles' first Christmas away from home. On December 26 the Polish soldiers left by train for France, which pleased the captain of the *Ardeal* because he would not have to feed the ninety men during the many idle days in port that lay ahead. It actually took two weeks to unload the grain in Genoa and then prepare the ship for departure, and the Poles would not complete their Mediterranean journey to Marseilles until January 8, 1940.[47]

CHAPTER FIVE
Sojourn in France

When the *Ardeal* arrived in Marseilles, the commander of the police immediately sent a detachment to the harbour to guard the Polish national treasures. The captain of the *Ardeal*, who hadn't given a second thought to the value of the shipment of metal trunks his vessel had carried from Romania, was amazed at the importance being attached to them. He had entertained no idea of the value of his cargo. Arrangements were made very quickly to send the treasures on to Aubusson, a city in central France. They were to leave that same day, escorted by an inspector of the Police Mobile who would be accompanied by one of the Polish workmen.[48] During this time in Marseilles the weather was warm and it rained continuously; consequently, everyone engaged in inspecting the trunks and getting the shipment under way was soaked to the skin. Polkowski and Zaleski stayed in a hotel overnight and left by train the following day. On the way to Aubusson it turned very cold, with the temperature dropping to minus-17 degrees Celsius. The French railway coaches were unheated, and Polkowski complained bitterly of frostbitten feet.[49]

In Aubusson the national treasures were destined to be housed at the Mobilier National (National Furniture Depository), where they would be placed with the French State Art Collection that had already been moved there from Paris.[50] Aubusson was a safe haven away from industrial areas that might be threatened by aerial attacks. Moreover, the town had been a centre of tapestry weaving since medieval times and the Mobilier National continued to maintain an enterprise there for tapestry making and repair. This was certainly an excellent location in which to store and care for the Wawel tapestries — and indeed for the safekeeping of the entire Polish national collection.[51] Once Polkowski and Zaleski had arrived in Aubusson, the cases containing the Polish treasures could be transferred from the railway station to the Branquerie storage facility by hand cart. The curators found the management at the Mobilier National most kind. They helped the newcomers in every way they could.[52]

For three days the curators unpacked the items they had accompanied on the long journey from Cracow. The articles were carefully shelved and a detailed inventory was prepared. The only problem that they discovered involved one of the long metal tubes that housed the tapestries. This case had somehow developed holes that had allowed water to get in and subsequently freeze, damaging some of the valuable arrases. The staff of the Mobilier National offered to repair the damage and to clean away the mould that had developed due to the dampness. The work was beautifully done and the Polish government-in-exile paid for the expenses. Once the inventory was complete, the lists were checked against the Wawel inventory book which had been brought from the castle. Everything tallied exactly and Zaleski was able to take a copy of the inventory to the Polish government which was now located in Angers, the former capital of the province of Anjou, about 200 kilometres northwest of Aubusson.[53]

In the three weeks that passed before Zaleski returned from Angers, Polkowski and his two assistants began the task of cleaning all the arrases. With the help of equipment borrowed from the Mobilier National, dust and dirt were removed and they were taken outdoors, unfolded, and spread out on the snow to air.[54] There seems to have been some measure of disagreement between Polkowski and Zaleski concerning the best way to carry out repairs to the tapestries. Zaleski favoured the Austrian school of restoration, which held that only materials contemporary with the arrases should be used, thus preserving historical authenticity. These would have to be obtained from discarded tapestries of that time period. Polkowski, on the other hand, having received his education at the Moscow School of Fine Arts, upheld the views of the Russian school, which maintained that the purpose of any restoration was to make the tapestry appear as the original artist had intended. If modern materials and techniques could best accomplish this, they should be used. Polkowski argued that the use of centuries-old, neglected thread or yarn left the arras dull in colour and structurally weaker.[55] This rather fundamental dispute was never resolved. However, when he returned from Angers, Zaleski brought with him instructions to the effect that Polkowski was to remain with the collection until the necessary conservation work was complete, presumably around the end of March. Zaleski himself only stayed in Aubusson about a week before leaving to establish himself in Paris. As the restoration work progressed at Aubusson, it soon became clear that the methods of the Russian school would prevail in the workshops of the Mobilier National.[56]

By March 28 the conservation work had been completed and Polkowski had also made his way to Paris.[57] There, an art historian from Cracow, Dr. Karol Estreicher, had been placed in charge of an office that was investigating the fate of Polish national art objects.[58] Swierz Zaleski was already working for Dr. Estreicher, who now undertook to find employment for Polkowski as well. Polkowski's new job turned out to be the conducting of statistical analyses for another government department, at which he worked for an hourly wage. About this time Zaleski left the pension where he had been staying and rented a small apartment, which contained an art studio, in the Montparnasse district. He told Polkowski that in France he had found the aim of his life, the rebirth of an interest in fine arts. Rather than devote his time to the Polish art treasures, he preferred to paint in his new studio and exchange ideas with other Parisian artists in the cafés they frequented.[59]

According to Polkowski, Zaleski visited him one day to complain about the way he was being treated by the Polish government-in-exile. It would seem that Vice President Kot was insisting that he do the work that had been assigned to him in Estreicher's office. Kot told Zaleski that since he had nothing to do in Aubusson, he should spend his time at his place of work in Paris instead of loitering in coffee houses during working hours. Zaleski started to go to work for two or three hours a day, but after a short time Estreicher suggested that it would be better for him to stay home, as he was only distracting others from their work.[60]

* * *

At this time conditions seemed almost normal to those living in central France. This was the period of the "phony war" in western Europe. British and French troops had not budged to attack the Third Reich in September 1939 when Hitler's troops overran Poland. The western powers had declared war against Germany, but nothing happened. The same leaders who had given away Czech territory at Munich in 1938 in order to appease the Führer — Edouard Daladier in France and Neville Chamberlain in Britain — were still in place. Were they still more intent upon appeasing the German dictator than upon pursuing their joint war effort? The French had mobilized a huge army of eighty-four divisions, but they seemed determined to remain strictly on the defensive behind their Maginot Line, which they felt would keep the enemy at bay. The British had sent an expeditionary force of 160,000 men to northern France to help man the French defences, but still nothing happened. Barrage balloons floated over the city of London, sandbags were unloaded to protect important buildings, and windows and street lights were blacked out against air attacks. Despite a sense of impending danger, the war seemed unreal for most people.

All this came to an end on April 9, 1940, when the Nazi juggernaut was unleashed against Denmark and Norway without a word of warning in an unprovoked attack. The Danes had little choice but to surrender as the German army rolled across their unfortified frontier. The Norwegians held out longer; although all their major ports had been seized by the Germans within forty-eight hours, they went on fighting from their rugged terrain, which made resistance feasible. In the north, around Narvik, they held out for several weeks.

The next major German attack was launched against the Netherlands, Belgium and Luxembourg on May 10 — again without warning, again unprovoked. Within four days most of Holland was in Nazi hands. Two weeks later the Belgian king surrendered his country to the Germans, and tanks were rolling into northern France. By moving through Belgium, the German army had outflanked the "invincible" Maginot Line and was heading toward Paris. In two short months the war picture had changed drastically. This was indeed blitzkrieg — lightning war.

CHAPTER SIX
On the Road Again

The events on the war fronts of western Europe led to great consternation among the Polish exiles in France. On May 17, after the invasion of Belgium and Holland, the office where Polkowski worked moved from Paris to Angers. Jozef Polkowski stayed behind to obtain the documents he needed to travel. While he was still in Paris, he met Zaleski in a café at dinnertime, which surprised him greatly as he knew that Zaleski had received a written order from Vice President Kot to proceed to Aubusson and prepare the collection for evacuation. The next day, his documents in order, Polkowski left for Angers, where he was to work on the documentation of Polish government funds that were to be evacuated from France.

On June 9 the vice president telephoned Polkowski to ask about Zaleski's whereabouts. When he replied that he was probably in Aubusson, Polkowski was ordered to send a telegram to make sure. Two days later a letter arrived from one of the Polish workmen stating that Zaleski had arrived in Aubusson on June 1 to collect his salary and had left again for Paris that same day. Extremely angry, Kot placed Polkowski in charge of the collection with orders to proceed to Aubusson as soon as the necessary passports were ready and to pack the collection for evacuation. In the meantime a messenger was sent to Paris by motorcycle with an order for Zaleski to report immediately to Angers. The motorcyclist found Zaleski's apartment occupied, a fact the concierge confirmed, but he could not gain admittance and had to leave his message under the door.

Polkowski left Angers for Aubusson at dawn on June 13, travelling by private car to Limoges and then by bus to Aubusson. Much to his surprise he found Zaleski at the local hotel they frequented. He had arrived earlier that same day, travelling by truck from Paris with a consignment of articles from the Polish embassy — valuable objects, but nothing of historic importance. Zaleski admitted he had received the message placed under the door of his apartment, but flatly refused to obey any orders issued by Kot. Besides, in his view, the Germans would never enter Paris or Aubusson, so he was planning to make the return trip to the French capital the next day. Unfortunately for Zaleski, his driver refused to undertake the trip back to Paris. Upon approaching the railway office, he was told that train tickets in that direction were no longer available. Zaleski was devastated as he had left all his possessions, including his art supplies, in his Paris apartment.

After a day of consultation with the French authorities at the Mobilier National, packing started on June 15. Because many of the metal cases in which the treasures had been brought from Cracow were no longer in good condition, it was decided to ship all the tapestries in packages. They were to be first wrapped in thick waterproof paper and then sewn up in heavy canvas by upholsterers from the Mobilier National. The arms, armour and other precious objects were placed in five of the metal containers that were still serviceable. On that same day Dr. Estreicher arrived by car with three valises containing valuable historic objects that had been dispatched to Aubusson by order of the Polish council of ministers. They were to be added to the Wawel collection, along with which they were to be treated with the greatest of care. Estreicher had no inventory of the contents of the suitcases, and Polkowski accepted them as they stood without opening them. The war news was grave enough that there was no time to waste on the niceties of documentation.[61]

When the contents of the valises were examined much later, they were found to contain many extremely valuable items, such as the coronation sword of the last Polish king, Stanisław Augustus Poniatowski, as well as an aquamarine sceptre and a chain of the Order of the White Eagle which had also belonged to him. Most valuable of all the articles rescued that day were the ancient Polish manuscripts. The oldest items in the collection were the Annals of the Holy Cross, written in Latin between 1122 and 1136, and the Chronicle of Wincenty Kadlubek,

Bishop of Cracow, which told the story of events in Poland up to the year 1206. Considering that the art of reading and writing had only been introduced into Poland by Christian monks around 1000 A.D., these were indeed early manuscripts. Also present were fragments from the thirteenth-century Sermons of the Holy Cross, the very first writings in the Polish language, and the earliest translation of the psalms into Polish, the Florian Psalter from the fourteenth century. In addition the collection contained several illuminated Books of Hours and some works of secular literature such as the courtly poem "Le Roman de la Rose," as well as the prayer book of Queen Bona, the Italian wife of King Sigismund I, the sixteenth-century ruler who had modernized the old medieval castle on the Wawel Hill. Only two items among the entire collection of books did not belong to the National Library of Poland: a sixteenth-century psalter and an extremely valuable Gutenberg Bible printed in two volumes between 1453 and 1455. These belonged to the library at the seminary of Pelplin, a small town located south of Gdansk near the Vistula River.[62]

Equally important was a collection of Chopin manuscripts and memorabilia, treasured by the Poles as mementos belonging to a national hero of the nineteenth century, that dark period in Polish history when foreign powers had occupied the land. Frédéric Chopin had been born near Warsaw in 1810 and spent the first twenty years of his life in Poland. With his Polish-French heritage he had easily made the transition from occupied Poland to Paris, a city where many other Polish émigrés had gathered. Although he never returned to his birthplace, Chopin never forgot his Polish heritage. The mazurkas that he wrote in Paris reflected the rhythms and tunes he had heard in the Polish countryside, while his polonaises mirrored a more formal, courtly Polish tradition. Found among the collection were twenty-three original handwritten copies of mazurkas, nocturnes and other pieces, together with printed copies of several compositions autographed by Chopin. The collection was also supposed to include three daguerreotypes of the composer as well as a number of letters written to him.[63] These manuscripts and memorabilia had been purchased by the Polish government in 1937 from Breitkopf and Hartel in Leipzig, the original publisher of Chopin's works. They were first placed with the Chopin Institute in Warsaw, which turned them over to the National Library one year later because it could better look after the collection.[64] Together the materials constituted a musical treasure of great value not only to citizens of Poland but to the music world at large.

When the threat of war intensified in early 1939, all these artifacts were located in Warsaw. Both the Chopin material and the early manuscripts were in the National Library, while the royal regalia of Sigismund Augustus was on display in Warsaw's Royal Castle. On August 5 they were moved to the basement of the Bank of National Resources (Bank Gospodarstwa Krajowego) in the same city. Then, in September, they were evacuated with the property of the bank into Romania. From there they reached France on September 26 and were placed first in the Polish embassy and then in the Polish Library in Paris.[65] It was from there that Estreicher had retrieved these historic objects in order to transport them to Aubusson on orders from the government-in-exile.

* * *

The war news Dr. Estreicher brought to Aubusson was indeed desperate. According to him, the German forces were approaching the outskirts of Paris. Actually, the Germans had entered the city the day before, on June 14, the day when Zaleski had been desperately trying to make his way back to his Paris apartment. Because of these developments the Polish government had decided to move from Angers to Libourne, not far from Bordeaux, where access to sea transport could be obtained. In view of the war reports, the Polish government sent orders that the entire collection of Polish national treasures was to be evacuated from Bordeaux as quickly as possible. Jozef Polkowski had learned from local Polish workers of a used truck that they might be able to purchase, and Estreicher provided the money to carry out the transaction. Everything was packed and ready to go by ten o'clock the following morning, but they still did not have a driver who was prepared to undertake the 250-kilometre journey from Aubusson to Bordeaux. It was not until evening that one of the Polish workmen appeared with a Spanish communist*

---

*During the Spanish Civil War (1936–39), the communists had fought with the loyalist forces of the Spanish government against General Francisco Franco who had the necessary licences required to drive throughout all France. When this Spaniard agreed to take on the trip, Polkowski refused to let him out of his sight. He paid for the driver's dinner, took him straight to the truck thereafter, and at 10:00 p.m. they were on their way.[66]

Stopping at Libourne the next afternoon to consult with the Polish government, they were told by Vice President Kot that the French had requested an armistice. As a result of this news the vice president told the curators to drive straight to Bordeaux and to board any ship sailing for England, where the entire Polish government would shortly be moving. By 4:00 p.m. they had reached Bordeaux, where the Polish consul advised them that Captain Gora of the Polish freighter *Chorzow* would provide their passage. The next few minutes, as described by Polkowski, were full of excitement:

> In a short while the captain drove up, listened to the consul's story and, without saying anything, took us with him. He sat next to our driver to guide him, and we drove to the port. When we approached the gate, the captain ordered the driver to press down on the accelerator. At full speed, in spite of the yells of the guards, we reached the place where the *Chorzow* was anchored. Here the captain called the whole crew and told them to carry our goods at lightning pace to the hold, whilst we were told to hide. When finally the guards came running up, the truck was empty and to the questions of the guards as to why we did not stop, the captain replied that because the truck was empty he saw no need to stop, since here he had urgent things to do.[67]

That evening they were joined on the ship by a few dozen Polish airmen and a number of civilians with their families. The airmen were

and his nationalist rebel army. With the support of Italy and Germany, General Franco gained the upper hand in the fighting. When the armies of the Spanish Republic surrendered to Franco in March 1939, many of the loyalists crossed the border into France as refugees — Spanish communists among them.

placed at the bottom of one of the ship's holds, where they would be out of the sight of prying eyes, while the other passengers made out as well as they could on the open deck. In the daytime the trunks containing the Polish treasures and the large packets of tapestry were used as chairs and tables, while they served as beds at night. Because of the crowding, Captain Gora was well aware that food was going to be scarce, so he ordered everyone ashore to find their own sustenance for the voyage. They departed with orders to be back at 4:00 p.m. since the ship was scheduled to depart at six that evening (June 17).[68]

The *Chorzow* sailed in the tail of a large convoy. At midnight, off La Rochelle, they were awakened by gunfire and the explosions of bombs. When the ship next to theirs sustained a direct hit, the curators of the Polish treasure removed Szczerbiec, the medieval coronation sword, from its packing case. They were determined to rescue at least this one symbol of their heritage. Nothing further untoward happened to them that night, and the next morning Captain Gora decided to leave the convoy and make a run for England on his own. He figured that he could make twice the speed of the slow-moving convoy, and in this way he hoped to slip past the coast of France undetected. Very soon they were out on the open sea enjoying glorious weather, and in two days they reached Falmouth without further incident.[69]

The *Chorzow* was not allowed to dock until the following day, June 22. While the passengers awaited permission to enter Falmouth, shifts changed in the dockyard. The port workmen, struck by the faces of the tired and dishevelled children, organized a party of men who went into town and returned in about half an hour with lots of hot tea and sandwiches. The food kept coming until a hundred Polish refugees had eaten — hospitality that was much appreciated. Around midday two buses arrived to take the soldiers and civilians into town. Polkowski stayed behind alone to guard the state treasures. Around five o'clock an officer from the British Admiralty arrived with an order for the captain of the *Chorzow* to sail for France immediately. The captain protested that he could not leave without unloading the valuable cargo he had brought from France. The officer secured a railway freight car to take the treasures to the station and used British dock workers to load the collection onto the railway carriage. The British railway authorities managed to get this baggage car attached to a passenger train that was leaving for London that night, and Polkowski and Zaleski purchased the necessary tickets to travel to London on the same night train.

Word of their departure had been sent on ahead to the Polish embassy in London, so an embassy official was waiting to meet them at the station when they arrived the next morning. This gentleman placed an additional embassy seal on the baggage car and sent the two curators off to a London hotel. On the next day the national treasures were removed from the station and placed in one of the drawing rooms at the Polish embassy.[70]

Conditions on the war front had not improved one whit. On June 21 a new French government headed by Marshall Pétain had signed an armistice with the Germans. All of northern France, as well as the Atlantic coastal area, were to be occupied by the Germans, with the French government retaining control of a block of territory in southeastern France bordering on the Mediterranean Sea. These developments left Britain and its Commonwealth to carry on the fight against Nazi Germany alone. Only twenty-one miles of sea separated Hitler's victorious forces from the British Isles, and an invasion from the continent was expected very soon.

Under these circumstances the Polish national treasures could hardly be considered safe on British soil. But where could they be moved next? The Polish government-in-exile began negotiating with officials from the Canadian High Commissioner's Office in London for permission to send the collection across the Atlantic to Canada. There is no record of proceedings on the London side of the high seas, perhaps because the discussions were carried on face to face or by telephone. We do know, however, that on June 24 and July 11 Wiktor Podoski, the Polish consul in Ottawa, contacted the Department of External Affairs in the Canadian capital about these matters. In his correspondence Podoski mentioned the ongoing conversations between the London Poles and the Canadian High Commission. The negotiations concerning the departure were apparently completed by July 1, since the Polish curators took steps to obtain the necessary Canadian visas on that date.[71]

The Polish treasures, unopened during their stay in London, left for Glasgow in a sealed baggage car on the afternoon of July 2. Polkowski and Zaleski travelled north that same night. The next day everything was loaded aboard the Polish ship SS *Batory* in the harbour at Greenock, northwest of Glasgow. At 5:30 a.m. on July 4 they started out in convoy for Halifax. The convoy consisted of the SS *Bermuda*, a British ocean liner that was transporting British refugee children to Canada for the duration of the war, as well as three Polish ships: the *Batory*, formerly a transatlantic liner and the flagship of the Polish merchant marine; the *Pilsudski*, sister ship to the *Batory*; and the *Levant*, a much smaller cargo vessel. Guarding the convoy as it set out was the battleship *Revenge* along with a cruiser and two destroyers, all of them Royal Navy ships.[72]

During their first day at sea an aeroplane launched by catapult from the *Revenge* spotted a German U-boat. One of the destroyers immediately began to circle the commercial ships, all of which stopped their engines. The destroyer dropped a number of depth charges about fifty yards from the *Batory*, the resulting explosions being strong enough to shake things up aboard the Polish vessel. This must have frightened away the U-boat; after about fifteen minutes things quieted down and the convoy continued on its way. When Polkowski asked why they had so strong an escort for their transatlantic voyage, a British naval officer explained that there were many German U-boats in British waters. Two days before, the Germans had sunk two British ships that were actually carrying 2,500 German and Italian prisoners of war bound for Canada. This time, the passengers aboard the *Bermuda* were British children, a cargo valued much more highly. An anecdote from Polkowski's account of the next day's experiences reinforces these comments:

> The following day a large number of passengers who were not affected by sea sickness observed a great quantity of some huge fish near the *Batory*, showing off their enormous carcasses. Lieutenant Winkler told me that we were just passing near the place where two days before the ships with the prisoners of war had been sunk. And as usual on such occasions the sharks had gathered for a meal. This information was not too pleasant.[73]

Before long, the two Royal Navy destroyers returned to Britain, having fulfilled their duty as escorts through the U-boat-infested waters around the British Isles. The next day, unfortunately, the *Pilsudski* developed engine trouble that forced it to stop. The commander of the convoy ordered the RN cruiser to stay behind as a guard for the crippled Polish vessel, leaving only the battleship *Revenge* to escort the convoy on the rest of its way across the Atlantic.[74]

At about this time in Ottawa, Podoski was writing his second letter to the External Affairs department, a letter containing more specific information about the Polish ships that were on their way to Canada. He requested admission to Canada for a number of refugees, the families of Polish government officials and of army, navy or merchant marine officers. All of these people possessed Canadian visas or had received permission to enter the country from the Canadian High Commissioner in London. In addition, Podoski requested free entry into Canada for the Polish national art treasures from the Wawel Castle, for a wireless station destined for the Polish embassy, and for several cases of documents from the archives of the Polish embassy in London.[75] The Polish consul must have had complete confidence that these requests would be favourably received, since the ships in question had already crossed the Atlantic and were approaching Canadian waters.

The convoy was soon met by Canadian destroyers that accompanied the ships on the rest of their voyage. They arrived in Halifax on July 12, one week and one day after their departure from Scotland, after a relatively uneventful crossing. Not so the *Pilsudski*. The Poles learned some time later that their sister ship had been sunk in mid-Atlantic as she lay crippled, a sitting duck for enemy submarines.[76]

Hussar's armour with feathers,
seventeenth century.

Velvet hat and cloak, both given to King Jan Sobieski in recognition
of his defeat of the Turks at Vienna in 1683.

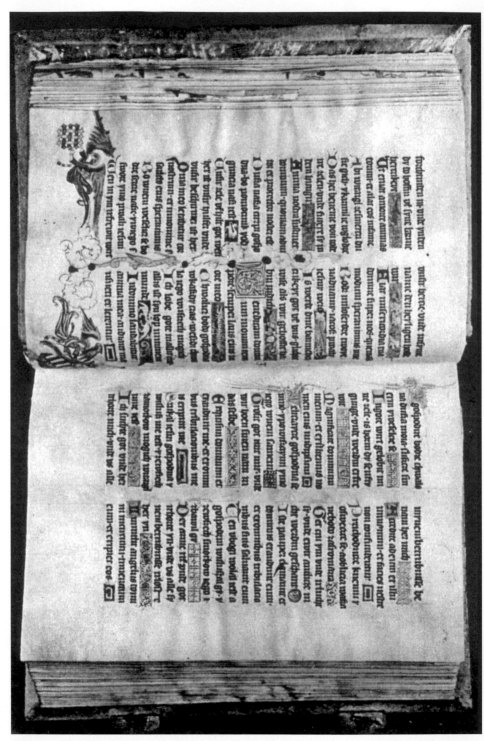

Florian Psalter, fourteenth century. It contains the earliest translation of the psalms into Polish.

Illumination from
the missal of Bishop
Erasmus Ciolek, 1522.

Illumination from
the Book of Hours,
fifteenth century.

Gutenberg Bible, 1453–1455.

Chopin manuscript, Fantasy in B-flat Major, Opus 61, nineteenth century.

CHAPTER SEVEN
Canada — A Safe Haven

When the transatlantic convoy docked in Halifax Harbour on July 12, 1940, trains — guarded by dozens of railway police and Royal Canadian Mounted Police — waited alongside to transport a very special cargo. It was only then that Jozef Polkowski learned the convoy had carried a large shipment of British and Polish gold bullion to safety in Canada. Now the gold was being transferred to railway coaches for the journey to Ottawa, a task that took top priority and therefore received immediate attention from the railway authorities. Because the floor of each baggage car would only support the weight of 150 to 200 boxes of gold ingots, five trains were required to convey this record shipment. Locked inside each railway car were two guards on four-hour shifts, fifty guards in all attached to the convoy. The bullion travelled uninsured, since no one would venture to underwrite such a vast amount of gold in wartime. The shipping costs charged by Canadian National Express apparently set another record in this amazing transatlantic adventure. Now Polkowski understood the real reason for the strong naval escort that had accompanied their merchant ships across the Atlantic.[77]

Thanks to the intervention of the Polish consul general and the Canadian Department of External Affairs, the Polish treasures were allowed to enter Canada duty free as the property of the Polish government.[78] On the night of July 13 the transfer of the treasures to Canadian National Railway coaches was complete and the collection left Halifax under the protection of the RCMP. The two Polish curators travelled on the same train, and when the mounted police officers invited Polkowski and Zaleski to use the restaurant car on the train as their guests, the two men gratefully accepted. This gesture of hospitality absolutely astounded Polkowski, who was certain that nothing like it would ever have been extended back home. When the train arrived in Ottawa on the morning of July 15, the curators organized the transportation of the collection to the Polish consulate, where it was temporarily lodged in the basement of the building.[79]

The Polish treasures could not remain in the cellar of the consulate indefinitely, and so the Polish consul general began to make inquiries as to where he could find more suitable accommodation. Podoski first approached Dr. H.O. McCurry, the director of the National Gallery of Canada. McCurry was sympathetic, but he could do little for the Polish consul since his own institution was operating under very crowded conditions in shared space within the Victoria Museum at the foot of Metcalfe Street. He advised Podoski to contact Dr. Gustave Lanctot, the director of the National Archives of Canada. During a conversation with Podoski on July 24, Lanctot suggested that he could find space for the Polish national treasures in the Records Storage Building at the Department of Agriculture's Experimental Farm. The building had been erected especially for the storage of valuable documents and was therefore fireproof, with suitable temperature and humidity controls. The two curators visited the building the next day and found the site eminently suitable.[80]

By August 2, arrangements had been finalized through correspondence between Podoski and Lanctot. In a letter written on August 1, Podoski said in part:

> Thanks to the attitude of the Canadian Government and particularly to your efforts, Sir, the Polish nation will now have its souvenirs placed in an allied shelter, after having been saved at the cost of so much difficulty and after having been carried across so many countries and so many seas.
>
> It is understood that the articles in question will in no way involve the responsibility of the Canadian Government, since they have not been placed in its hands.

On the contrary, it is the undersigned who, as the representative of the Polish Government, accepts full responsibility for the space which was placed at his entire disposal for the period during which the articles will be stored.

I hope that this arrangement ... will be agreeable to your Government....[81]

Lanctot replied the following day, noting Podoski's declaration that "the Polish Government assumes full responsibility for the period during which these articles will be in safekeeping" and assuring him that the Canadian government agreed to this arrangement. [82]

Initially, the chests and packages containing the treasures were placed on the floor of a large, completely empty room that occupied one entire floor of the building.[83] A request to the Department of Public Works led to the installation of metal shelves along the walls for storage and metal tables for restoration work on the royal tapestries, as well as an overhead rod stretching the entire length of the building from which the tapestries could be hung.[84] Once these installations had been completed, the unpacking of the collection could commence. Everything seemed to be intact, although the textiles were full of dust and dirt, leaving much work to be done.[85] For security reasons a new lock with four available keys was placed on the door of the large room that held the treasures. Polkowski and Zaleski were each given a key, since the Poles had assumed responsibility for the collection. The other two keys went to the janitor of the building and to the RCMP, which kept a round-the-clock guard on the Public Records Building.[86]

Polkowski and Zaleski had barely begun unpacking at the Records Storage Building when they found themselves caught up in Canadian regulations. The National Registration Act required adults in Canada to register between August 19 and 21 so that the government could assess the best use of available manpower in the face of the wartime emergency. The two curators registered in Ottawa at Polling Station #110 on August 21, supplying information that provides an interesting thumbnail sketch of each of these Polish citizens who had only just arrived in Canada.

Aside from the usual statistics about place and date of birth, Jozef Polkowski declared that he spoke three languages — French, Polish and Russian — but no English. He held a university degree as an architect-engineer. His health was fair. He was employed as the guardian of the Polish records and archives dispatched to Ottawa. This was not his usual occupation, but he had held the position for one year. Polkowski had been raised on a farm, where he lived until the age of sixteen. He had worked on the farm for four of these years and could milk cows, but he could not handle horses, drive a tractor or use farm machinery. Polkowski indicated that he would like to be trained in horticulture and that he would also appreciate the opportunity to learn English. As for military service, he had served with both sappers and engineers in the Russian and Polish armies between 1914 and 1920, holding the rank of lieutenant. He left the army as a result of demobilization.[87]

Stanisláw Zaleski had been born in Cracow in March 1886, which made him fifty-four years old in 1940 — two years older than Polkowski. He spoke French and Polish, but no English, and he had a Ph.D. from the Jagiellonian University in Cracow. Like Polkowski, Zaleski was married. As far as his health was concerned, he reported that he was myopic but that, generally speaking, his health was good. He stated that he was working as a conservator of the Polish records and articles that had been sent to Canada, a continuation of work he had been doing in Poland for fifteen years. He had neither experience in farming nor in industry, but reported that he could work as an artist or college professor. Zaleski also stated that he had served in the Polish armed forces for dates that proved unreadable. Most likely this occurred during the Soviet invasion of Poland in 1920.[88]

* * *

Once the two men were established and had sorted and stored away the various objects in the collection, the next step was to carry out a formal inventory. Everything that had been removed from the Wawel Castle in September 1939 checked with the inventory prepared in Aubusson, France. The medieval manuscripts and other objects that had come from Warsaw and had reached Aubusson just before the evacuation were also checked. Because the keys to the three valises were missing, their locks had to be broken open. This having been done, the contents were found to correspond with the lists provided by the National Library in Warsaw and by the Polish Library in Paris, where they had been stored for some time.[89]

To look after the cleaning and repair of the tapestries, two Polish women who had emigrated to Canada before the war were hired. Because many of the tapestries required extensive repair work, women with special skill in weaving were required.[90] Mrs. Kozlowska was the wife of an employee at the Polish consul general's office and Mrs. Sliwkowa the wife of the chairman of the Ottawa Polish Club. They started work on September 6 for the meagre wage of two dollars for each eight-hour day, a sum they accepted because of the slender resources available to the Polish consulate in Ottawa. Initially, the ladies found that they could not work for a full week because they needed some respite to allow tired muscles to relax.[91]

The tapestries had not been unrolled for more than a few hours since the departure from the Wawel Castle. It was now possible to hang them for a period of two weeks from the long rod installed in the workroom so that they could be aired properly and get their creases shaken out. Thereafter the arrases were kept on metal shelves, which had been outfitted with a curtain that could be drawn to shut out the light.[92] While they were in Aubusson, the technicians at the Mobilier National had recommended reinforcing the arrases with a linen backing to prevent them from sagging, so Mrs. Kozlowska and Mrs. Sliwkowa now proceeded to attach great sheets of linen to the backs of the tapestries.[93]

Ed Sliwka, a tall teenager who frequented the Records Storage Building at the Experimental Farm in those years, was the son of the seamstress who was working on the Wawel tapestries for the Polish curators. He attended Ottawa Technical High School and lived with his family in their duplex on Grove Avenue. From time to time he visited the storage building and helped with the treasures. Sliwka can remember squirting Three-in-One oil onto a piece of cheesecloth in order to polish the grey, nicked blade of Szczerbiec, the ancient coronation sword of the Polish kings. The weighty sword was definitely a two-hander, according to Sliwka, who also remembers an ancient saddle that needed softening with leather balm, as well as a very long cape with an ermine collar — a cape so long that it would have covered a man *and* his horse. He also recalls his mother working for weeks in the dining room of their home to repair a much-damaged tapestry.[94]

* * *

In February 1942, another cache of Polish national art treasures arrived in Ottawa. These artifacts had been sent to the United States to adorn the Polish pavilion at the 1939 World's Fair in New York. Most prominent among these exhibits was a collection of six suits of medieval armour from the State Museum at Kornik, a small town near Poznan in western Poland.[95] The collection included a complete set of seventeenth-century armour for rider and horse — chain-mail shirt, helmet, shoes, pistols, armour for the horse, and one wing from a hussar's* imposing feather regalia, which would have been worn into battle attached to his shoulders.[96] After the World's Fair had closed, these artifacts were transferred by the Poles to the Metropolitan Museum of Art on the understanding that they could be removed on six months' notice.[97]

Proper notice must have been duly given, as Polkowski left Ottawa for New York on December 14, 1941, to collect the Polish armour. The first hurdle he faced was that of getting the items through customs. After ten days of negotiation it was agreed that the Polish government could reclaim these items, duty free, for shipment to Canada. In the meantime, American museums had received instructions to pack away their valuable items in the wake of the Japanese attack on Pearl Harbor on December 7 and the U.S.'s subsequent declaration of war on Japan,

---

*The hussars were the seventeenth-century Polish heavy cavalry. These warriors wore two great arcs of eagle feathers mounted on their backs and rising well over their heads. Each rider was helmeted and plumed, and each of them carried a twenty-foot lance with streaming pennants. They must have been a formidable sight as they charged across a battlefield with the feathers on their backs creating an evil hiss while the ground shook beneath them with the pounding of their horses' hooves (Zamoyski: *The Polish Way*, p.3).

Germany and Italy. Confusion over these instructions to the museums caused another delay. By this time, Polkowski was getting desperate; the armour still had to be packed for shipping and the entire transaction needed to be completed before January 5, when his visa expired. The deadline was met, as Polkowski left New York in due time and reached Ottawa on January 6.[98] The armour followed in late February.[99]

The question of financing all these activities was a constant source of concern for the curators of the treasures. When they left France, Polkowski had been given $2,000 to cover the costs of the journey. He had managed to keep all of this in reserve and to bring the entire sum with him to Canada. With these funds, he and Zaleski had managed to operate for their first six months in the country. The curators themselves lived on salaries of $100 each per month, and as we have seen the Polish women who worked repairing the tapestries received a pittance.[100] Since many of the original chests had been damaged during the months of difficult travel, new ones had to be purchased for the delicate fabrics and the valuable objets d'art made of gold and precious metals. The Experimental Farm was located on the very outskirts of the city in those days, and the two curators found that daily travel was an expensive proposition. Another interesting entry that appeared amongst each month's receipts was the sum of $10 for cigarettes. Apparently, these were used to tip government employees who worked at the Records Storage Building for their help in lending tools and carrying out various tasks around the premises.[101] The curators' salaries were raised — first to $125 per month and then to $150 by 1943 — but no one was living luxuriously in wartime Ottawa on salaries like these.[102]

During these years while Polkowski and Zaleski carried out their tasks at the Records Storage Building, very few people in Ottawa were aware that so much of a nation's heritage was being housed on the outskirts of their city. However, the two curators and the Polish consul general did entertain some of the senior public employees who were privy to the secret. Dr. McCurry, the director of the National Gallery, came with his secretary, Miss Fenwick; Dr. Lanctot, director of the National Archives, attended with his wife; and Colonel Archer Duguid and Lieutenant Commander Alan Beddoe of the

Historical Section, Department of National Defence were on hand as well. The Poles took pride in showing their guests the many marvellous objects that were housed in the Records Storage Building.[103]

* * *

At this time in the early 1940s Ottawa was a very different city from the capital we know today. In the heart of downtown the Parliament Buildings, centred by the Peace Tower, still dominated the skyline. Government office buildings were low-rise stone structures, built to blend in with the Gothic, château-like style favoured in the capital. These structures were rapidly being supplemented by temporary buildings erected on any available downtown space to house the many civil servants hired to deal with the exigencies of war. Railway tracks still ran down the east side of the Rideau Canal to Union Station opposite the Château Laurier, making access to the heart of Ottawa much easier for travellers from out of town than it is today.*The War Memorial at the head of Elgin Street had just been unveiled in 1939 by King George VI, and a stone's throw away the new Lord Elgin Hotel had opened its doors in 1941. At that time, Lord Athlone was governor general, and he lived at Rideau Hall; but no official residences had yet been provided for the prime minister of Canada or the leader of His Majesty's Loyal Opposition. William Lyon Mackenzie King, Canada's wartime prime minister, lived at Laurier House in the Sandy Hill area, a residence bequeathed to him by Lady Laurier, the widow of former prime minister Sir Wilfrid Laurier. Kingsmere, in the Gatineau Hills north of Ottawa, was King's private summer retreat, its lawns adorned with stone ruins collected by the prime minister from buildings being demolished in the Ottawa area and beyond. In the nearby hills, winter sports enthusiasts skied at the Ottawa Ski Club's Camp Fortune, the only such facility in the Gatineau. This was the Ottawa of the 1940s — compact, serene, comfortable, replete with green parkways, and rather provincial and introspective in its outlook.

At first, life in the city of Ottawa would not have been very easy for Jozef Polkowski and Stanisláw Zaleski. Polkowski reported that, early

---

*The station is now a federal government conference centre.

on, the language barrier was considerable. He began to learn English by reading newspapers with the help of a dictionary and by listening to some of the English-speaking boarders in the house where he lived. Finances were never easy, but Polkowski supplemented his earnings as curator by working at the Experimental Farm from time to time. In Ottawa at that time there was no Polish parish to which a newcomer could turn for help, but Polkowski did meet some local Poles, and he was invited to join the Polish-Canadian Club, most of whose members were older Poles who had settled in Canada long before the Second World War. Although he did not often travel outside the city, Polkowski did establish another connection by visiting Barry's Bay, a community near Algonquin Park where Polish immigrants had settled. Only after some years in Ottawa would Polkowski get to know a number of Canadians, some of whom became his good friends.[104]

Zaleski could not speak English any better than his fellow curator, although he too managed to make friends in Ottawa over the next few years. Zaleski seems to have once more busied himself in the field of fine arts during his sojourn in Canada. In 1942 he helped the Polish legation organize an exhibition of contemporary Polish art at the National Gallery in Ottawa, producing the catalogue for the show himself. In his preface Zaleski commented on the development of Polish art in the twentieth century, thus putting the works in context. The exhibition ran from March 25 until May 4 at the National Gallery and was visited by a record number of people, including General Sikorski, the head of the Polish government-in-exile, who happened to be visiting Ottawa. Thereafter the paintings were shown in a number of other Canadian cities until the tour finally ended in October 1943. Zaleski must have been well satisfied with his contribution to this very successful exhibition.[105]

The two curators were well-educated officials from the upper echelons of the Polish civil service. In 1940 they had found themselves new arrivals in a city where they could not participate in the kind of cultural life they had enjoyed at home. Each had left behind a wife and son about whom they had received no news. Their homeland had been invaded and occupied by Germany and Russia in 1939, then overrun by German troops when they attacked the Soviet Union in June 1941, and again by the Russian army in its counterattack against Germany later in the war. What was happening to their family and friends? What would ultimately be the fate of their country? These concerns must have weighed heavily on the minds of the two men as they endeavoured to adjust to the language and customs of a new country.

CHAPTER EIGHT
The Fortunes of War

In 1939 the Poles fought valiantly against the German juggernaut that swept across their frontier on September 1. It had been agreed in talks with the British and French general staff that the Polish army would hold down the German forces for two weeks, giving the French time to launch an attack against the German Rhine frontier. By September 14, however, Warsaw was encircled by the Wehrmacht. The city held out for another fortnight, but no French soldiers moved from their Maginot Line defences on the German border. The French and the British had indeed declared war on Germany in support of their Polish ally, but not one offensive was mounted by the western Allies in September 1939 while the Poles struggled desperately to fend off German invaders.[106] The Royal Air Force restricted its operations to the dropping of propaganda leaflets on German cities. Could this have been because the same statesmen in London and Paris who had undertaken to appease Hitler at Munich in September 1938 were still in charge?

The Polish military tried to regroup its forces in the south and east in the Lwow area, but on September 17 Russian armies invaded Poland from the east, intent on seizing their share of the spoils of war. The continued defence of southeastern Poland was no longer feasible, and the last scattered Polish forces capitulated over the next three weeks. Once more the country had been overrun by its large neighbours to the west and east, and an independent Poland had ceased to exist. The Germans had at least paid dearly for their victory, losing more than 50,000 men and close to 700 planes and 900 tanks and armoured cars. This was greater damage than they would sustain in the fighting for the Low Countries and France in the spring of 1940.[107]

In October, Poland was divided between Germany and the Soviet Union. The Russians occupied a number of provinces stretching along their frontier, from Wilno in the north to Lwow in the south. In western Poland the Germans annexed West Prussia, the area around Poznan, and part of Silesia. This left a block of territory in central Poland to be run by the newly created General Government. These lands, which included the cities of Warsaw and Lublin as well as Cracow in the south, were ruled as a German colony by Hitler's friend Hans Frank. The Germans declared that the concept of Poland was to be wiped from the human mind. Almost immediately members of the Polish intelligentsia — priests, teachers, lawyers, mayors — were picked up and incarcerated in the concentration camp that had been established at Auschwitz. These people were potential leaders of resistance against the new regime and could not be allowed to survive. Those Poles who were not earmarked for extermination were to serve as slave labour for the German master race.[108]

Despite these German threats, Polish participation in the Allied war effort did not end with the formal capitulation of September 28, 1939. In France, a Polish army of 85,000 men was formed from escapees arriving from eastern Europe and émigré Polish volunteers from France and the United States. After the fall of France in June 1940, the Polish forces regrouped in Britain. By 1945 there were over 200,000 soldiers in the Polish army, an effective air force boasted ten fighter squadrons and four bomber squadrons, and a navy of sixty vessels was involved in the Battle of the Atlantic. Poles fought alongside the Red Army on the Russian front, with the British Eighth Army in North Africa, and in the Italian campaign, where the Polish Second Army Corps under General Władysław Anders* took Monte Cassino

---

*Arrested by the Russians in 1939, General Anders spent two years in the infamous Lubianka prison. When the Germans attacked the Soviet Union in 1941, an agreement was reached between the Poles and the Russians to end the state of war between their two nations. Anders was released and he began to assemble a Polish army to fight alongside the Russians. After considerable harassment by the Russian authorities, Anders decided to take his army out of

after very heavy fighting in the area. When the main fighting front shifted to France after the D-Day landings on the Normandy beaches, the Polish army took part in the fighting in western Europe that helped to bring about the final collapse of the Third Reich.[109]

Meanwhile, back in their homeland, the Polish underground forces formed the largest contingent of clandestine fighters on the continent. The AK (the Army Krajowa or Home Army) had been organized by a group of senior Polish officers at the time of the Polish capitulation in 1939. By 1944 the AK numbered close to 400,000 men, operating under the control of an underground executive based in Warsaw. Across Poland the AK blew up bridges, derailed trains and cut communication lines. Inside factories where Polish slave labourers manufactured war equipment for the Germans, representatives of the AK sabotaged engines and navigation equipment destined for German tanks, guns and planes. In addition the Warsaw underground executive organized clandestine law courts and elementary schools, as well as the "flying universities" that operated despite a German ban on such educational activities. In Warsaw, hardly a national holiday went by without the Polish national anthem being broadcast by the AK over the official German loudspeaker system. All this despite the fact that death awaited anyone suspected by the Germans of belonging to the Polish underground.[110]

By the summer of 1944 the Red Army was sweeping across Poland. On July 27 Russian forces had crossed the Vistula River about 50 kilometres south of Warsaw, and Russian guns could be heard in the city. Two days later, advance units had reached a point only 15 kilometres northeast of Warsaw. All this posed a serious dilemma for the leaders of the AK, who desperately wanted to liberate Warsaw themselves before the Russian troops arrived. The Polish government-in-exile advised

---

the U.S.S.R. to Iran, where he joined the British forces that were operating there. From Iran the Polish troops went on to fight in the North African campaign and then to participate in the invasion of Italy. At Monte Cassino the Germans had fortified the Benedictine monastery atop the 500-metre hill very heavily. For six months they held this ground and prevented the Allied armies from advancing up the Italian peninsula. Under General Anders' leadership the Poles ended this long and bitter stalemate with their breakthrough in May 1944. (Zamoyski: *The Polish Way*, pp. 361–2)

against an uprising, stressing that the AK could expect no assistance from the Allied forces in the west. It did, however, concede that the final decision should rest with the underground leaders on the spot. After consulting with his fellow officers, the commander of the AK made his decision: the uprising would start the following day.

At 5:00 p.m. on August 1, the AK went into action all over Warsaw, seizing control of large sections of the city but not managing to take the airport, the main railway station or any of the bridges that crossed the Vistula River. By August 6 they had been fought to a standstill, and thereafter they could only defend themselves. This they did in magnificent fashion for a total of sixty-three days. The Luftwaffe dive-bombed the parts of the city the Poles controlled, while German artillery poured in the shells. As the Germans advanced from the western suburbs, street by street and house by house, they slaughtered civilian inhabitants as they went. Very little outside aid reached the beleaguered AK fighters. Allied planes flying from northern Italy did drop supplies on the night of August 4, but the round-trip flight of 2,500 kilometres made the venture a very costly one for the Allied air crews. When the western leaders requested landing facilities behind the Soviet lines, Stalin refused. The Allied long-range airlift continued, but many of the supplies meant for the AK fell into German hands as the sections of the city under Polish control diminished. At the same time, on the eastern edge of the city, the Russian forces did nothing. Instead of continuing its advance westward, the Red Army pulled back from the outskirts of Warsaw, and the sound of Russian artillery could no longer be heard on the streets of the city.

After four weeks of bitter street fighting, the AK commanders in the Old Town decided to evacuate their 4,000 men through the sewers to the city centre. There the fight continued for four more weeks. Finally, on October 2, the military command in this last pocket of resistance signed a capitulation agreement. There seemed little point in prolonging the agony. The AK fighters were treated like regular soldiers and were accorded all the rights of prisoners of war. Warsaw's civilian population, however, was herded into cattle cars and removed from the ruined city. As soon as they had departed, SS demolition experts proceeded to destroy any buildings left intact.

There was nothing left but rubble when the Red Army finally "liberated" Warsaw in January 1945.[111]

All military activities by the AK underground in Poland or the regular Polish army in western Europe were carried out under the authority and control of the Polish government-in-exile in London. When the Polish army had been forced to capitulate to the Germans in September 1939, Poland's president and the remainder of the government had crossed the southeastern frontier into Romania. From there they had taken refuge in France and, after the fall of France, in London. This government-in-exile was recognized by the Allies as the legitimate government of Poland, a recognition that was extended to the Polish government even by the U.S.S.R. after the Nazi invasion of Russia in 1941. The civilian government consisted of a National Council made up of representatives of all the major Polish political parties. The chairman of the National Council was Stanisław Mikolajczek, while General Wládisláw Sikorski served as premier and commander-in-chief of the Polish armed forces. After Sikorski's untimely death in an airplane crash at Gibraltar, Mikolajczek became prime minister.[112]

* * *

During 1944 conditions began to change drastically for the Polish government in London, as its position as the sole representative of the republic was undermined by the rapid advance of the Red Army across Poland. In January the Russian forces crossed the 1939 boundary between Poland and the U.S.S.R.; in April they liberated Lwow; and by July they were in Lublin. On July 22, 1944, a group of Stalin's client Poles established a Polish Liberation Committee in Lublin. By this time Stalin was refusing to negotiate with the Polish government-in-exile unless changes were made to its composition. The Polish prime minister, Stanisláw Mikolajczek, flew to Moscow at the end of the month. Despite grave misgivings Mikolajczek agreed to the establishment of a provisional government for Poland with a majority of its members drawn from the Lublin Liberation Committee. Mikolajczek accepted these one-sided arrangements only because of Stalin's intransigence and because of pressure from his British and American allies[113] — after all, it was the Red Army that was in place on Polish soil.

On January 5, 1945, the Soviet Union recognized the new provisional government as the legitimate government of Poland and broke off relations with the Polish government in London, which had refused to ratify the arrangements made by Mikolajczek in Moscow.[114] At the Yalta Conference in February the western powers agreed to Stalin's demand that Poland's frontier with the U.S.S.R. should follow the Curzon Line, some 200 kilometres to the west of the 1939 boundary. Poland was to be compensated with German territory in the west (see Map V — Poland 1945). With respect to the establishment of a Polish government, the report on the conference stated:

> A new situation has been created in Poland as a result of her complete liberation by the Red Army. This calls for the establishment of a Polish Government which can be more broadly based than was possible before the recent liberation of western Poland. The provisional government which is now functioning in Poland should therefore be reorganized on a broader democratic basis with the inclusion of democratic leaders from Poland itself and from Poles abroad. This new government should then be called the Polish Provisional Government of National Unity.... This Polish Provisional Government of National Unity shall be pledged to the holding of free and unfettered elections as soon as possible on the basis of universal suffrage and secret ballot. In these elections all democratic and anti-Nazi parties shall have the right to take part and to put forward candidates.[115]

This "Provisional Government of National Unity" was organized by early June; sixteen of its twenty-one ministers were Stalin appointees, and the head of the Lublin Liberation Committee was named prime minister. Mikolajczek was to serve as deputy prime minister in the new government.[116]

The United Kingdom and United States recognized the new Polish government on July 5. Canada followed suit the next day, withdrawing its recognition of the Polish government in London and notifying the legation in Ottawa of the change in policy. To follow closely in the footsteps of its two senior partners in the Atlantic Alliance was obviously standard Canadian foreign policy at that time.[117] And so the London-based Polish government-in-exile, which had struggled valiantly for five and a half years to maintain a Polish presence among the fighting allies, was being bypassed for political reasons. Such were the fortunes of war.

CHAPTER NINE
Missing Treasures

After the Canadian government recognized the new Polish regime, it took several months before the Warsaw Poles put together a new team to represent the nation in Ottawa. The head of the Polish mission was Dr. Alfred Fiderkiewicz, a medical doctor who had worked in the United States before the outbreak of war.[118] Fiderkiewicz was a lean, bald man with bushy eyebrows and an intense, perhaps even commanding, expression.[119] Once he had become an established figure on the Ottawa scene, the Polish diplomat acquired the nickname "Fido" among the members of the diplomatic corps — an appellation that was not exactly complimentary, but undoubtedly convenient.[120] Dr. Zygmunt Bielski served as first secretary of the Polish legation and also as chargé d'affaires in the absence of Dr. Fiderkiewicz. There were, in addition, three Polish consuls serving various Canadian cities, and a cultural attaché in the person of Professor Edmund Semil. This completed the delegation sent to Canada by the Polish Government of National Unity in Warsaw. Besides representing Polish interests in Canada, the mandate of the new delegation included the recovery of $17 million worth of gold ingots and, even more important, the Polish national treasures that had been deposited in Ottawa in 1940. Before his departure from Poland, Dr. Fiderkiewicz called on the Polish premier, Edward Osobka-Morowski, and on Deputy Premier Wládysláw Gomulka. Both leaders emphasized the importance of arranging for the return of these invaluable national properties.[121]

The Polish delegation departed by ship. Upon reaching Britain, however, Dr. Fiderkiewicz and his wife took a plane to New York to visit their two sons, who were living in the United States. The rest of the legation continued their journey by sea, arriving in New York toward the end of April 1946. From there, Dr. Bielski went on to Ottawa to arrange accommodations. Before long, the Polish government purchased two Ottawa properties: one on Carling Avenue, which was to house the Polish legation, and the other on Stewart Street. Until these transactions could be completed, however, temporary quarters would have to suffice.

At the beginning of May, Dr. Fiderkiewicz arrived from New York. He was met at the airport by the chief of protocol for the Department of External Affairs, who drove Fiderkiewicz and his wife to the Château Laurier, which was to be their temporary residence. The Polish minister was received on May 2 by Norman Robertson, the undersecretary of state for External Affairs, who welcomed him to Ottawa. They only exchanged a few words on this occasion because the Polish minister had not yet officially presented his credentials to the Canadian government, a cere-mony that was not scheduled to take place until the end of the month.[122]

In the meantime, the new Polish minister set out to discover the whereabouts of the Polish national treasures as the first step toward reclaiming them for his country. Fiderkiewicz began his inquiries by inviting the two curators to meet with him at the Château Laurier on May 16. Fiderkiewicz received them as if they were his best friends. He regretted that he could not drink a proper toast with them because his Polish vodka had not yet arrived. He spoke about their mutual friends in Cracow and described the things that he had done as the first post-war mayor of that city. Commending them for their efforts in shepherding the Polish treasures to safety in Canada, he spoke of his present concern for the return of the items to Poland. As the three men got beyond the pleasantries and turned to more serious matters, however, the discussion did not run smoothly.[123] The interview therefore proved frustratingly unproductive for Fiderkiewicz. Polkowski refused to disclose any infor-mation concerning the whereabouts of the national treasures. Before their departure, however, Zaleski did indicate that he would like to return and speak further with Fiderkiewicz, and this second interview was arranged for the next morning.[124]

* * *

In order to understand what was taking place, it is necessary to backtrack several months to 1944–45, when the Red Army was advancing across eastern Europe and had established in Poland an alternative regime to the Polish government-in-exile in London. This meant that those Poles in Canada who had had positions of responsibility conferred on them by the London government faced a difficult choice. Were they to maintain their allegiance to the Polish government in London, or should they lend their support to the new regime? In 1939 Zaleski and Polkowski had undertaken their perilous journey across a Poland overrun by invading forces. They had been threatened by German armies from the west and by Russian forces from the east, but they had been determined not to let the important artifacts in their care fall into foreign hands. Now the German forces were in retreat, but the Russian army had returned to Poland. What sort of homeland was about to emerge? Would it be safe to send the national treasures back to Poland? If not, what should be done with them?

The two curators saw things very differently. Polkowski refused to consider repatriation. He recalled what had happened in 1795, when Poland had been partitioned and obliterated from the map of Europe. At that time, Russian soldiers had seized the Flemish tapestries of Sigismund Augustus, the very tapestries that they had rescued with so much difficulty in 1939. The Russian army had taken them away to adorn the palaces of St. Petersburg, and there they had remained throughout the nineteenth century. Polkowski very much feared that this same kind of plunder might occur again. Zaleski, on the other hand, had more faith in the Russians and the Lublin Committee they had established. He argued that, under the Treaty of Riga in 1921, it was the communist regime in Russia that had authorized the return of the Flemish tapestries to Poland, setting to rights the crimes of its czarist predecessors. Zaleski therefore did not think the Russians were about to abduct them again twenty years later.[125]

At this time — that is, in 1944 — Dr. Wracláw Babinski headed the Polish legation in Ottawa. He had been appointed to that post by the Polish government-in-exile in London, and to that government he was responsible. Born in 1887, Babinski had obtained his doctorate in Social and Economic Studies in 1910. At the end of the First World

War he had joined the newly established Polish Foreign Ministry and had helped set up Poland's consular services around the world. He became the Polish minister to Canada on August 31, 1944, when Wiktor Podoski retired from that position to return to London. As events evolved in Europe during 1944, Babinski watched the Polish situation with concern. When the Russian government recognized the communist-dominated Lublin Committee as the legitimate government of Poland on January 5, 1945, he became increasingly alarmed, fearing that recognition by the rest of the Allied governments, including Canada, would quickly follow. He was determined that the Polish national treasures should not fall into the hands of a communist-controlled regime. The art treasures would have to be removed from the Public Records Building at the Experimental Farm as quickly as possible. But where could they be stored?

Dr. Babinski consulted with the two curators, who were involved on a daily basis with the care and supervision of the treasures. He first suggested removing the national treasures to the small Polish community of Wilno, Ontario, about 150 kilometres west of Ottawa. The parish priest there, a friend of Babinski's, had agreed to store the treasures in the basement of the Roman Catholic church. Both Zaleski and Polkowski, however, objected vigorously to this proposal, arguing that the wooden church building presented a fire hazard.[126]

Becoming increasingly desperate, the representatives of the London Poles decided to deposit their most valuable artifacts with the Bank of Montreal. Sorting through the many articles housed in the Public Records Building, they selected enough small objects to fill two large steamer trunks. These prize artifacts included the ancient coronation sword Szczerbiec, several early manuscript chronicles of the Polish nation, the Gutenberg Bible, the coronation regalia of King Stanislas Poniatowski, and the Chopin manuscripts, as well as a coffee service and a number of goblets fashioned out of gold. The two trunks, carefully packed, were taken to the Sparks Street office of the Bank of Montreal on March 2, 1945, and were deposited in the vault. The trunks were registered as the property of Dr. Stanisláw Zaleski and Jozef Polkowski, both of whose signatures would be required to secure their release.[127]

77

Dealing with the Wawel tapestries and the other large objects in the collection did not prove quite as simple. Babinski approached a number of Roman Catholic religious authorities in Quebec, through the good offices of the Polish consuls in Montreal and Quebec City. Ascertaining that space was available at the monastery of the Redemptorist Fathers in Sainte-Anne-de-Beaupré near Quebec City, Dr. Babinski secured the approval of the primate of Quebec, Cardinal Jean-Marie-Rodrigue Villeneuve, for the use of the monastery for storage purposes. The two custodians then visited Ste. Anne and met with Father Léon Laplante, the superior general of the Redemptorist Fathers. They found the storage arrangements very satisfactory. The Polish treasures were to be placed in two large, well-ventilated rooms that were reasonably fireproof, and the curators were given permission to visit the monastery from time to time in order to carry out any necessary preservation work. Accordingly, twenty-three trunks and one wooden case were sent to the monastery on May 21, a detailed list of their contents being forwarded to Dr. Babinski.[128]

Babinski, however, was not prepared to move all his valuable assets into the same place. Looking around Ottawa for another safe location, he was offered space at the Convent of the Precious Blood on Echo Drive.* When Zaleski and Polkowski examined these premises, they concluded that a new wall would have to be built and a door sealed up before the artifacts could be housed there securely. This work was duly undertaken and eight trunks were moved to the convent in June 1945. The vast majority of the articles that were placed at the convent were military pieces — saddles and harnesses for war horses; armour, shields and helmets; and pistols and sabres. The shipment also included one portrait, a seventeenth-century clock manufactured in Torun, and the hat donated by Pope Innocent XI to King Jan Sobieski for his services to the Christian world at the siege of Vienna in 1683. The receipt for the Polish treasures was signed by two of the sisters from the convent and by Zaleski and Polkowski. One copy was kept at the convent and

---

*The convent has since been closed and the buildings demolished. The chapel of the Convent of the Precious Blood was carefully dismantled and rebuilt at the National Art Gallery on Sussex Drive in Ottawa.

the second was turned over to Dr. Babinski, together with a list of the artifacts that had been deposited at the convent. The first secretary of the legation, Adam Zurowski, then suggested that a password be established to identify anyone requiring access to the treasures. "The Holy Virgin of Czestochowa" (Matka Boska Czestochowa)* was chosen as the designated password, and Dr. Zaleski communicated the key phrase to the convent authorities and to Polkowski.[129]

Thus, almost twelve months before Alfred Fiderkiewicz arrived in Canada, most of the Polish treasures had been quietly removed from the Records Storage Building at the Experimental Farm and sequestered elsewhere. The few objects that remained on site were obviously the least valuable items from the collection. This was the amazing story that Stanisláw Zaleski told Dr. Fiderkiewicz when they met for the second time on the morning of May 17, 1946.**

---

*The monastery of Jasna Gora at Czestochowa in southern Poland possesses the sacred painting *The Black Madonna* — *the Holy Virgin of Czestochowa*. Over the centuries the Black Madonna came to be recognized as the "queen" of Poland whose special powers have come to the rescue of that country in some of its darkest hours. Pilgrimages to Czestochowa on the special Marian festivals in the church calendar have become an important tradition for Catholic Poles.

**All the actions carried out to hide the treasures by Dr. Babinski, Polkowski and Zaleski were undertaken before Canadian recognition was withdrawn from the Polish government in London on July 6, 1945. The three men were, therefore, legitimate representatives of the legal government of Poland, entrusted with the sole responsibility for the safekeeping of the Polish treasures while they were in Canada. When they chose to remove the national treasures of Poland out of the Records Storage Building, they were acting entirely within the law.

CHAPTER TEN
The Canadian Response

On the afternoon of May 17 Norman Robertson, Canada's under-secretary of state for External Affairs, received an urgent phone call. Dr. Alfred Fiderkiewicz was requesting an immediate interview. This was an unprecedented undertaking by the new Polish minister. Because he had not yet presented his credentials to the governor general at Rideau Hall, he was not an officially accredited member of the Ottawa diplomatic corps and had no right to approach the External Affairs department. Nevertheless, the case being urgent, call he did and the interview was granted. Once seated in Robertson's office, Fiderkiewicz reported a disaster. Practically all the national treasures belonging to Poland had disappeared from the Records Storage Building at the Experimental Farm. Robertson was astounded.[130]

* * *

The first indication of concern over the well-being of the Polish national treasures had come from the office of the British High Commissioner* several months before. On January 26, a Mr. Bell of the High Commission telephoned External Affairs to report that the

---

*The term "high commissioner" was the official name of the British minister to Canada. The position dates back to 1880, before Canada had its own diplomatic representatives abroad. At this time the Canadian government decided that it would be advantageous to have a delegate in London who could represent Canada's interests. The title of high commissioner was coined to designate the representative of the Dominion of Canada to the U.K. and eventually the representative of the U.K. to Canada. The term is still used today.

British had been instructed to take possession of any belongings of Dr. Wracláw Babinski's legation and hold them in safekeeping for ultimate delivery to the new Polish minister to Canada. These items were expected to include office furniture and files, a radio transmitting station, and "some Polish art treasures that are being held somewhere." Bell knew nothing about these two latter items, but Babinski agreed to provide an inventory of his official possessions. The British wondered whether it might be more suitable for the Canadian authorities to take over the possessions of the legation in Ottawa and indicated that they were prepared to do whatever the Canadian External Affairs department thought appropriate. Robertson's initial reaction was that it would be preferable to let the British complete the liquidation of Polish business in Canada, and that message was telephoned to Bell.[131] External Affairs would soon discover that avoiding responsibility with regard to the Polish national treasures would not prove to be that easy.

At this time, the Department of External Affairs seems to have been completely unaware of the presence of the invaluable Polish treasures in its country. When asked by a visitor about the Polish tapestries from the Wawel Castle earlier in January, Robertson confessed that he did not know of their existence.[132] Even four months later, when the new Polish minister from Warsaw had been in Ottawa for some two weeks, another member of the department indicated that he was unaware that there were Polish treasures in Canada.[133]

This lack of awareness is perhaps not so surprising when one considers the situation carefully. In July 1940 External Affairs had arranged with the port authorities in Halifax for the entry into Canada of Polish personnel, equipment for a wireless station, Polish art treasures and several cases of confidential documents — all brought to Canada on the Polish motorship *Batory*. Subsequently there was much correspondence concerning the establishment of a wireless station at the Polish embassy in Ottawa, but not one further word about art treasures. The arrangements for storing these artifacts at the Records Storage Building in Ottawa were negotiated by the Polish consul general with Dr. Gustave Lanctot, the director of the National Archives of Canada, rather than with External Affairs. Copies of the correspondence between these two gentlemen were forwarded to External Affairs. Then silence reigned. The Polish curators continued their conservation work on the treasures at the Records Storage Building, with the occasional Canadian visitor, but none from External Affairs.[134] Moreover, it is important to remember that this was wartime Ottawa; there were other matters than Polish national artifacts occupying the minds of Canadian civil servants on Parliament Hill. In addition, the war years must have seen many changes of personnel within the External Affairs department, disruptions that continued into 1945 and 1946 as readjustments to civilian life took place.

Before the Second World War, foreign affairs had never been a major concern for most Canadians. Canada had established its Department of External Affairs in 1909, but recognition that the Dominion of Canada might develop a foreign policy independent of the British government in London was a long time coming. Canada sent its first representative abroad in 1927, when Vincent Massey became its minister to Washington. Massey was a minister, not an ambassador, and he supervised a legation rather than an embassy; the terminology was carefully designed not to offend "British sensibilities," whether in the United Kingdom or among the many anglophiles living in the Dominion of Canada itself. Shortly after Massey's appointment to Washington, Canadian legations were established in France and Japan, and there matters rested until 1939. During all these years the fledgling department was supervised directly by the prime minister of Canada, and there was no Canadian minister of External Affairs. The first appointment of a cabinet minister to manage the department did not come until September 1946, when Louis St. Laurent was made secretary of state for External Affairs.

* * *

Bell's aforementioned phone call about Polish property initiated a flurry of activity within the Department of External Affairs. Approaches were made to Dr. Lanctot and Dr. McCurry of the National Gallery to see what information they could impart. By January 28 P.T. Molson of External Affairs had reported that he had tracked down the arrival of Polish goods in Halifax in July 1940. He went on to say that he had found no trace of the art treasures but that he thought some of them might be at the Polish legation. Two days later, Molson was able to report on the arrangements that Lanctot had made to store the art treasures in the Records Storage Building at the Experimental Farm.[135] Then, on February 2, R.G. Riddell reported to Robertson a "curious situation" that existed in regard to the treasures. Access to that part of the government building where they were stored was available only to the Poles themselves. In addition, Dr. McCurry of the National Gallery had told him privately that there was some doubt in the minds of these Poles about the wisdom of handing over the treasures to the new Polish government in Warsaw.[136] By the end of April the department had determined that the Canadian government possessed no inventory of the Polish art treasures.[137]

It was in that same month of April that Dr. Babinski submitted his promised inventory of Polish property to the British High Commissioner. Mr. Bell of the High Commissioner's office reported to External Affairs that the list contained no reference to the Polish art treasures. Bell felt that the matter had become "very delicate." The Canadian undersecretary, in a note appended to this report, wrote that the matter should be cleared up before the arrival of Dr. Fiderkiewicz, who was expected in Ottawa very soon.[138] Obviously, this had not happened.

* * *

On that afternoon of May 17 when Dr. Fiderkiewicz hastened to consult the External Affairs department, Norman Robertson might have been surprised at the new turn of events, but he was not unaware of the background of the affair. Robertson explained that Canada had never assumed any responsibility for the care and preservation of the Polish artifacts, a fact that had been carefully spelled out at the time of their arrival in correspondence between Dr. Lanctot on the Canadian side and Wiktor Podoski, the Polish consul general. Out of kindness to a wartime ally that had suffered disastrously, Canada had made space available for the storage of these Polish art treasures. The two curators who had shepherded the artifacts across Europe and brought them to this country remained solely responsible for them. They possessed the keys to the room where the articles were stored. The Canadian government had not even received an inventory listing the contents of the room.

Robertson did agree to tighten security arrangements at the Records Storage Building, and on that same day the Department of Public Works was instructed to install a new lock on the door to the storage area.[139] Later, on May 21, the RCMP were instructed not to allow anyone — neither the representatives of the London Poles nor the members of the newly established Polish legation — to enter the room where the Polish treasures had been stored without express permission from the External Affairs department.[140] These security measures were all very fine, but they did seem rather like locking the stable door after the horse had been stolen.

CHAPTER ELEVEN
The Search

When Dr. Fiderkiewicz notified External Affairs of the disappearance of the Polish treasures, he did not reveal all of the information at his disposal. Nothing was said about the three locations to which the treasures had been moved, nor about the defection of Dr. Zaleski. Fiderkiewicz was clearly playing for time in order to see what he could accomplish toward the recovery of the treasures by his own actions.

The obvious place to begin inquiries was in the city of Ottawa. The Bank of Montreal was likely to prove a hard nut to crack, since Polkowski and Zaleski were joint depositors of the two trunks left there and Polkowski was showing no interest in moving to the side of the Warsaw government. And so the Convent of the Precious Blood would be visited first. When Stanisław Zaleski and Edmund Semil (the cultural attaché at the Polish legation) called there on May 18, they were told by the mother superior that the articles in question had been moved from the convent by depositors who knew the required password.[141] Zaleski then travelled to Quebec City, where he got the same response from the Redemptorist Fathers: the cases that had been entrusted to their care were no longer on the premises.[142]

In the meantime, because Fiderkiewicz could not yet do so, Dr. Zygmunt Bielski, as first secretary of the Polish legation, had visited the External Affairs department three times to represent Polish interests. On the first occasion Bielski requested that the Canadian government take action to ensure that the Polish treasures not be removed from their current location without its permission.[143] On the second occasion (May 18) he reported that some of the missing treasures had been sent to Ste. Anne-de-Beaupré, and on his third visit (May 22) he stated that more of the treasures could be found in Ottawa at the Bank of Montreal and the Convent of the Precious Blood. He also said that Zaleski had visited Fiderkiewicz and had offered his cooperation in the search for the Polish treasures.[144]

Having received Bielski's information, the External Affairs department agreed to write to the organizations thought to be holding the treasures, asking them for a list of the Polish property deposited with them, the names of the depositors and the dates of deposit. In addition, these organizations would be requested not to part with the Polish property without first consulting External Affairs.[145] Between May 22 and 25 these letters were duly sent to the Bank of Montreal and the Convent of the Precious Blood in Ottawa as well as to the Redemptorist Fathers in Ste. Anne-de-Beaupré.[146]

The Bank of Montreal was first to respond. It reported that it had indeed received two locked steamer trunks on March 2, 1945, deposited by two Polish gentlemen, Dr. Stanisláw Zaleski and Jozef Polkowski. The bank agreed not to release these trunks without consulting External Affairs. Next, Mother Superior Marie de la Paix replied on behalf of the Convent of the Precious Blood. She stated that, six or seven months before, some refugees from Poland had asked to keep in the convent some trunks they could not store in Ottawa due to the scarcity of space. The sisters agreed to hold these articles and to deliver them only to duly iden-tified persons. The mother superior explained that because theirs was a cloistered order, neither she nor any of the sisters had seen the trunks at any time. Negotiations had been conducted through a small grille, and the articles had been stored in a basement room which the depositors could access through an outside door. A few weeks before, when duly appointed persons had come to reclaim the trunks that had been left, the sisters agreed to their request without further concern. Mother Superior did not know what had happened to the trunks after they had left the convent. Finally, on May 31, Father Léon Laplante answered rather laconically that there were no objects belonging to the Polish state at the Redemptorist monastery in Ste. Anne-de-Beaupré.[147] Once these replies had been received by External Affairs, the information contained there-in was passed along informally to the Polish legation through Dr. Bielski.

* * *

It was clear that the representatives of the London Poles had not wasted any time moving to protect the hidden treasures. After all, the steadfastness of Dr. Zaleski's loyalty to the London government-in-exile had been dubious even before the arrival of Dr. Fiderkiewicz in Ottawa. Zaleski had argued earlier, when the issue of returning the national treasures to Poland had been discussed, that there was no longer any risk in doing so. After Dr. Fiderkiewicz had arrived in New York, Zaleski was party to information about the new envoy's plans which he could only have received from someone in Fiderkiewicz's entourage.[148] And so, when the two curators went to meet Dr. Fiderkiewicz on the afternoon of May 16, the London Poles had a plan in place to deal with any emergency that might arise. Once Zaleski had agreed to confer with Fiderkiewicz again the following day, his intentions were obvious, as was the fact that the time had come to put that plan into action.

When Polkowski left the meeting, he returned quickly to his home, where Dr. Babinski was waiting in his car. By 7:00 p.m. the two men were on the road to Quebec City. They reached their destination at about eight o'clock the next morning and immediately started discussions with the highest church authorities in the vicinity about where to move the collection. Because certain key people were absent from the provincial capital, these negotiations took longer than expected. Finally, on written orders from the primate of Quebec, Father Laplante agreed to release the Polish treasures that had been entrusted to him. On May 23 they were removed — first to a nunnery at Ste. Anne-de-Beaupré and later to another well-hidden site in Quebec City.[149]

While Babinski and Polkowski were dealing with the situation in Quebec, a similar operation had been carried out at the Convent of the Precious Blood by other trusted members of the group. And so, before the end of May, the London Poles had the national treasures securely hidden once again.

* * *

By the end of the month the necessary documentation had finally arrived from Poland, and on May 31 Dr. Fiderkiewicz was able to visit the governor general, Viscount Alexander,* to present his credentials as Poland's minister to the Dominion of Canada.

With his status thus recognized, Fiderkiewicz was now in a position to send a formal letter to the External Affairs department seeking its assistance in recovering the Polish treasures along the lines suggested by Dr. Bielski in his earlier conversations.[150] Six weeks passed before External Affairs sent a reply to Fiderkiewicz. Again the department reiterated that the Canadian government had made space available in July 1940 for the storage of valuable Polish artifacts, but it had at no time accepted responsibility for the safekeeping of the treasures. The Canadian government sympathized with the desire of the Polish legation to recover the treasures, but it did not feel that it could assist the legation to secure the possession of treasures which had been stored by private arrangement in buildings that did not belong to the government.[151] Later in the same month, the secretary of state for External Affairs sent the Polish legation two keys for the room in the Records Storage Building where some of the Polish artifacts still remained. The RCMP had been advised to admit Dr. Zaleski and Professor Semil to the premises. Since they possessed the only two keys to the new lock that had been installed on the storage room, the legation was reminded that it was, as before, responsible for the articles deposited there.[152]

During the month of August, Dr. Fiderkiewicz made arrangements with the Bank of Montreal to have an inventory prepared of the various objects in the two trunks deposited there. On August 20 Zaleski and Semil were allowed into the vault in the bank in order to carry out this task. The two trunks still had the seals on them that had been placed on them before the trunks were deposited at the bank. Each of the seventy items was examined and replaced and the trunks were again sealed — this time with the seal of the Polish legation. This inventory of August 20, 1946, was then forwarded to the Polish Ministry of Foreign Affairs in Warsaw.[153]

---

*The governor general was the king's representative in Canada. Viscount Alexander was the last British governor general. He was succeeded in 1952 by Vincent Massey of the Toronto Massey family. All subsequent governors general have been Canadians.

Then, in September, Fiderkiewicz mounted one more attempt to interview Father Laplante of the Redemptorist Order at Ste. Anne-de-Beaupré. On September 5 he sent a very courteous letter to Laplante, requesting that Zaleski and Semil be admitted to the monastery to carry out conservation work on the Polish treasures. When the two conservators arrived in Quebec four days later, they found that Laplante had left for Aylmer the day before. They were received by Father Pelletier, who told them that the tapestries had been removed by individuals whose names he was not at liberty to disclose. Pelletier suggested that they could make further inquiries from Father Laplante in Aylmer, and so Zaleski and Semil travelled there on September 12. Laplante labelled Zaleski as a mere servant, and not a diplomat and former consul like Dr. Babinski, with whom Laplante was accustomed to dealing. He told them that the Polish treasures were no longer at Ste. Anne and that for any further information they would have to contact Cardinal Villeneuve. The next day, Fiderkiewicz wrote the cardinal, reviewing the sequence of events and requesting the cardinal's help in determining the whereabouts of the national treasures of Poland. On September 20 a reply came from the cardinal's secretary explaining that Villeneuve was in a New York hospital. The secretary promised to make further inquiries concerning the treasures, and a second letter followed ten days later. This time he stated that Cardinal Villeneuve had authorized Father Laplante to surrender the treasures to the gentlemen who had brought them to the monastery. This had indeed been done, but the cardinal knew nothing more about what had happened to them thereafter.[154]

By the end of September Dr. Fiderkiewicz must have been feeling quite frustrated with his lack of success in retrieving the national treasures of Poland. These were the most important historic artifacts that the Polish people possessed, embodying the history and traditions of their country. That was the reason they had been dispatched to Canada in 1940 for safekeeping. And yet here he was, the legitimate representative of the Polish state in Canada, charged with returning these historic objects to Poland, and in five months he had not even been able to locate the treasures. What approach should he try next?

* * *

Before closing this account of the search for the Polish treasures, it is important to return to the tension-charged days of May and June, when Dr. Zaleski had been behaving very strangely. The first evidence of Zaleski's agitated state occurred when he appeared at an RCMP post in Montreal on the morning of May 30, requesting police protection after claiming that his life was in danger. He claimed that the present Polish government would likely try to have him killed. The story is best conveyed in the statement made by Zaleski to the non-commissioned officer on duty at the police station that morning:

> Yesterday afternoon I took the train from Ottawa, arriving at Bonaventure Station at 6:00 pm. I slept on Dorchester Street, and today I am giving myself up to you to be executed and die.... I have a few dollars on me and $1,578.83 in the Ottawa branch of the Bank of Montreal. I am of the opinion that Mr. Polkowski is desirous of blackening me in the eyes of my superiors in order to destroy my reputation of honesty. I am all alone in Canada. My wife and son are still in Poland.[155]

Zaleski was later interviewed by the officer commanding the RCMP unit, who reiterated that Zaleski was afraid that he might be killed by the present Polish government if he could not produce the entire collection of art treasures. The officer commanding concluded that Zaleski's story was rather confused and should not be taken seriously. His assessment was that Zaleski was under some mental strain and could almost certainly be regarded as mentally unbalanced. He advised the gentleman to return to Ottawa and to consult his physician there which Zaleski promised to do.[156]

Instead of returning to Ottawa, however, Zaleski reported to a mental hospital in Montreal. On June 2 Jozef Polkowski received a telephone call from Mr. Brzezinski in Montreal, formerly the Polish consul there representing the London regime in that city. A doctor from the mental hospital in Montreal had contacted Brzezinski concerning a Dr.

Zaleski, who spoke neither English nor French and had come to the hospital seeking help. Brzezinski told the doctor that Zaleski spoke excellent French and sufficient English to communicate and suggested that he thought Zaleski was feigning madness.

When Polkowski heard this news, he agreed to try and get in touch with Zaleski the following day. When he telephoned Zaleski's Ottawa apartment, Polkowski found his compatriot at home. Zaleski refused to carry on a conversation, however, on the grounds that Dr. Fiderkiewicz had forbidden him to talk with Polkowski. That phone call marked an abrupt end to a relationship between the two curators that went back more than fifteen years.[157]

Polkowski supported the view that his colleague was faking mental illness — because he was afraid of being killed by communist agents after failing to restore the collection to Dr. Fiderkiewicz, and perhaps because, should he wish to renew his allegiance to the London side at any time, he might use mental illness as a device to explain that he had not known what he was doing during those troubled days.[158]

The RCMP's "A" Division in Ottawa continued to investigate Dr. Zaleski and his odd behaviour. Staff Sergeant Bayfield first interviewed Lieutenant Commander Alan Beddoe of the Royal Canadian Navy Volunteer Reserve, who had known Zaleski in the days when the Polish treasures were stored at the Experimental Farm. Beddoe stated that Zaleski was an art critic of high repute whose main concern was the preservation and return to Poland of the national treasures. Bayfield reported Beddoe's comments on his friend's recent behaviour in these words:

> On Thursday, June 13 last, Cmdr. Beddoe met Zaleski hurrying along Rideau Street without coat or hat during a heavy rain. At this time Cmdr. Beddoe observed that Zaleski was very nervous and looked quite ill. In conversation Zaleski stated that he had been having lunch in the Château Laurier and he observed some men watching him. He became afraid and had to leave as he thought they might kidnap or kill him. His speech was somewhat incoherent and it

was apparent he was under terrific mental strain. Cmdr. Beddoe offered to assist in any way I might suggest and he consented to accompany me should I decide to interview Zaleski.[159]

On the evening of June 19 Bayfield and Beddoe visited Dr. Zaleski at his place of residence. Zaleski stated that he had pledged loyalty to Dr. Fiderkiewicz when the latter arrived in Ottawa because he represented the recognized government of Poland. Zaleski thought that Fiderkiewicz would arrange to send the Polish national treasures home. After he had made this decision — this would have been around the middle of May — Polkowski and Adam Zurowski (the former first secretary to Dr. Babinski) tried to persuade him to remain with them. When he insisted upon upholding his new allegiance, Zurowski warned him that he would be punished. Worry about Zurowski's threat and concern about the treasures had preyed upon his mind to such an extent that he felt that he had to get away. It was for this reason that he had gone to Montreal on May 29. When Bayfield asked Zaleski if he still feared that some person might do him harm, he replied that their visit reassured him that he had nothing to fear. Bayfield commented that Zaleski had acted and talked in a perfectly normal manner at the time of the interview and that no further action needed to be taken by the RCMP.[160]

Whether Zaleski was faking symptoms of mental illness is not the primary issue. He obviously was deeply concerned about the decision he had made to transfer to the side of the Warsaw government. He had reported to Dr. Fiderkiewicz where the Polish treasures could be located, but nothing had been found at the convent in Ottawa, nor with the Redemptorist Fathers in Quebec. How would this affect his credibility with the Polish legation? Would his services be rejected by the new regime? The timing of the various developments leading to Dr. Zaleski's recovery is enlightening. On June 15 he received confirmation of his appointment as custodian of the Polish treasures from Dr. Fiderkiewicz.[161] Zaleski told Sergeant Bayfield on June 19 that he had resumed work at the Polish consulate and that the matter of the recovery of the treasures was being taken up by the legation in an official manner.[162] Zaleski felt fully recovered!

CHAPTER TWELVE
Questions Asked

To this point, the dispute over Poland's national treasures had been confined to the realm of diplomatic manoeuvring and ambassadorial niceties. That was about to change. On November 7 Dr. Fiderkiewicz called a press conference. The most complete coverage of the day's events is found in the Ottawa *Journal*, starting with a front-page report that began thus:

> The fabulous coronation sword of the Kings of Poland, "Szczerbiec," glinted in the rays of Ottawa's sunshine and a fortune in golden vessels and jewelled ornaments glittered and sparkled when, shortly after noon today, Polish Minister Dr. J. A. Fiderkiewicz descended into a locked room at the main office of the Bank of Montreal on Sparks Street and opened one of three trunks of Polish art treasures stored in the bank vault [actually, there were only two trunks stored there]....
>
> Flanked by burly guards, two official bank custodians and a group of newspaper photographers, Dr. Fiderkiewicz seemed filled with deep emotion when he stepped forward to break the seal on the plain steamer trunk that was brought into the room. The trunk ... was lashed with a few turns of heavy rope. The knot in the rope was sealed with a blob of red wax on which was the impression of the seal of the Polish legation, Ottawa.
>
> Slowly the minister lifted the lid. Almost nervously he pulled aside several paper-wrapped packages inside and

pulled forth what he had been seeking, the long, gleaming coronation sword of Poland. "Worth only a few dollars as so much steel and brass," he said, as he turned the blade in his hand, "to Poles, it is priceless." He pointed out the cross of Poland embossed on the blade and the pictures of Matthew, Mark, Luke and John inscribed on the hilt. There were also words in Latin.

He laid it down and brought forth a two-foot, mace-like, gold object with its heavy end, about the size of a large orange, completely encrusted with turquoises, emeralds and rubies. "This is the Hetman's Baton, the symbol of authority of the Polish field marshals for generations past." He could not estimate its value....

There were what appeared to be a large number of vessels, some apparently church ornaments, others royal dishes and drinking cups. Some were of gold, others of brass or bronze.[163]

The *Journal* printed four articles about the Polish national treasures in its November 7 editions. One report presented the initial reaction of the Canadian government as expressed by Prime Minister Mackenzie King himself. King told the press that the question of the missing treasures was not a government matter because the treasures had been kept in Canada as private property, adding that the Canadian government had had no control over these possessions. Other reports in the newspaper were based on interviews with Dr. Wracláw Babinski (the former Polish consul in Ottawa), the Redemptorist Fathers in Ste. Anne-de-Beaupré, and the Archbishop's Palace in Quebec City. Reporters were also searching for a man with a tumour behind his right ear who had been identified by the sisters at the Convent of the Precious Blood as the person who had removed the Polish trunks from their premises.

The story was big news. It was the first time the world at large had been given any inkling that Polish national treasures had been hidden away in Ottawa for the last several years — in itself, an admission that was startling enough. Now many of these precious historical artifacts had gone missing. This was indeed an eye-catching revelation.

* * *

The next day the *Journal* carried three more stories about the Polish treasures. According to the first report, the scarlet-robed mother superior at the Convent of the Precious Blood had spoken to a reporter from behind a grille at the sixty-year-old brick convent. She stated that the sisters had not been aware of the value of the Polish objects stored in their basement. The cases had been packed away in a store room and no one had paid any particular attention to them. Not being permitted to read newspapers, the cloistered nuns had not even heard the startling news that had broken in Ottawa about the Polish treasures until the newspaper reporter arrived at the door of their convent.[164]

Other reporters, who had been trying to track down the man with the tumour behind his right ear, had also met with success. The Polish man who fit this description was Jozef Polkowski, living at the home of A.F. Newlands, 29 First Avenue, Ottawa. The *Journal* reported:

> Joseph Polkowski, for 24 hours the mystery man of the still-unexplained disappearance of a rich collection of Polish art treasures, is a quiet, bushy-browed, middle-aged man who has definite opinions regarding responsibility for the loss.... He has a noticeable growth behind his right ear....[165]

The reporter went on to state that Polkowski denied he was the man who had withdrawn the treasures from the Convent of the Precious Blood. Polkowski admitted to making two visits to that convent with Zaleski, once to arrange their storage there and once thereafter. He also stated that he had made three visits to Ste. Anne-de-Beaupré, again with Zaleski — once to arrange the transfer of the treasures, once at the time of the transfer and once soon afterwards to air and examine the tapestries.

The third *Journal* story was based on a dispatch from the Canadian Press in New York. There, Cardinal Villeneuve reported through his secretary that he had never seen the Polish treasures that had been deposited with the Redemptorist Fathers in Ste. Anne-de-Beaupré. They had been reclaimed from the monastery there by a person with the proper credentials, but the cardinal had no knowledge of what had happened to them thereafter. Villeneuve, at the time of this statement, was in Misericordia Hospital in Bronx, New York, recuperating from a heart attack. Included with the story was a comment from Dr. Fiderkiewicz that he did not believe the Catholic Church was consciously hiding the treasures out of any ill will between the Polish government and the church. He asserted that the Catholic Church in Poland had all the privileges it had enjoyed before the war and he reiterated that he did not believe Poland had any quarrel with the church. Fiderkiewicz went on to say that he only wanted to see the treasures returned to their rightful place in Poland.[166]

Before long, the foreign press was aware of the events in Ottawa. *L'Humanité*, the communist newspaper published in Paris, carried a banner headline on November 9: "A Canadian Cardinal Has Stolen the Polish Treasure." The article suggested that to steal a billion and to insult the allied government that was being victimized was going a little far for a cardinal, even in Canada. It went on to recommend that the dispute be submitted to international arbitration at the United Nations.[167] Later in the month the Canadian embassy in Paris forwarded another article from a weekly publication called *Arts*, which the ambassador considered a respectable journal. This report stated that the Wawel tapestries must be returned to Poland. In order to accomplish this one had to know in what direction to search. The reporter then asked who had an interest in this larceny — and who could have been able to penetrate as far as the collections without arousing suspicion.[168] Pertinent questions indeed.

* * *

Five days after the press conference, Dr. Fiderkiewicz called on Lester Pearson, the undersecretary of state for External Affairs.* The Polish

---

*At this time Mackenzie King was the prime minister of Canada. Louis St. Laurent became Canada's first Secretary of State for External Affairs in 1946,

minister explained that he could proceed no further in his search for the missing treasures, having received no cooperation from the officials of the former Polish legation in Ottawa, nor from Cardinal Villeneuve, who had no information to impart to the Warsaw Poles. Under these circumstances, Fiderkiewicz had no choice but to ask for the help of the Canadian government in recovering the treasures. The Polish legation did not hold Canada responsible for the loss of the treasures, but the minister did feel that the Canadian government should help the legitimate government of Poland to recover state property that had gone missing on Canadian soil. Pearson replied that the Canadian government had exercised no control over the Polish treasures. Polish officials had possessed the keys to the storage area at the Records Storage Building, and they could have placed their property wherever they wished without consulting the Canadian government. He was not sure what the government could do, since it had accepted no responsibility for the articles under consideration.[169] The Department of External Affairs issued a press release later that same day informing the public of Dr. Fiderkiewicz's request for help in locating and restoring to Poland the national treasures of their country and outlining the Canadian government's response.[170]

On December 16 Pearson was presented with a very interesting proposal concerning the Polish treasures. He had asked Jozef Polkowski to call at the External Affairs department, and on that particular December day Polkowski appeared in his office, accompanied by L.W. Brockington, a prominent Ottawa lawyer who represented some of the London Poles residing in the city. Over the course of their conversation, Polkowski denied having anything to do with the removal of the treasures from the Convent of the Precious Blood or from the monastery of the Redemptorist Fathers. He also said that he had no knowledge of where the treasures had been placed. Then, after Polkowski had withdrawn, Brockington put forward a tentative solution

---

when that government department ceased to be operated from the Prime Minister's Office. Lester Pearson was serving as undersecretary of state for External Affairs, the top civil servant in the department, answerable only to St. Laurent, his cabinet minister. This situation lasted until King retired in 1948, whereupon the other two gentlemen moved one step up the ladder.

to the impasse that had developed. He suggested that those who had custody of the treasures should turn them over to the recognized Polish authorities, on the condition that they not be returned to Poland for a period of five or more years. During this intervening period the Polish treasures should be released to the Canadian government to be displayed publicly in Canada under the auspices of the Polish government. Brockington thought he could persuade his clients among the London Polish community to support such a plan. Pearson agreed that the proposal was well worth pursuing.[171]

Negotiations based on Brockington's proposals continued over many months. When External Affairs approached Dr. Bielski of the Polish legation with the plan, Bielski greeted the proposal with enthusiasm. It required more time to get the Polish government-in-exile in London to accede to the plan, but by May of the following year the Canadian High Commissioner could finally report that the London Poles had agreed to a settlement along the lines proposed by Brockington. At about the same time, External Affairs noted that the Polish legation had been very reasonable during all their discussions concerning the problem. A draft agreement was therefore being prepared by the department. This was where matters stood during the latter part of September 1947, when the General Assembly of the United Nations was scheduled to meet in New York. It was agreed that the Polish foreign minister would give his government's reply to the proposal to Louis St. Laurent, his Canadian counterpart, at that meeting. On September 25 the Polish minister told St. Laurent that the compromise that had been so painstakingly negotiated was completely unacceptable to the Polish government, bringing an abrupt end to the prospect of a settlement being negotiated.[172]

CHAPTER THIRTEEN
A Bird in the Hand

During the Second World War, the "Big Three" — Winston Churchill, Franklin Roosevelt and Jozef Stalin — had met several times to coordinate strategy, but after the collapse of Nazi Germany and the capitulation of Japan, the wartime alliance was showing signs of strain. The Soviets and the western Allies differed over the occupation of Germany and the composition of the new governments that were being established in eastern Europe. In March 1946, at a university convocation in Fulton, Missouri, Churchill spoke forcefully about the "iron curtain" that was being lowered across central Europe. From that point forward, the differences between the former wartime allies continued to intensify into the Cold war between east and west that was to dominate international politics for the next forty years.

In January 1947, Poland held its first national election since the war. At the Yalta Conference two years before, "free and unfettered elections" had been promised as part of the process of establishing a new Polish government. The largest political party at the time of the election was the Polish People's Party (PSL), whose 600,000 members numbered more than all the other parties put together. Its leader, Stanisláw Mikolajczek, had been persuaded to return from London to Warsaw and join the Polish Provisional Government that had been established in 1945. The second-largest party was the Polish Socialist Party (PPS), led by Jozef Cyrankiewicz, a pre-war political activist and survivor of the Auschwitz concentration camp. The party favoured by Stalin was the Polish Workers' Party, led by Wládysláw Gomulka. During the election campaign, one million citizens were disqualified from voting by bureaucratic manoeuvring; meanwhile, 149 PSL candidates were arrested and another 174 of its candidates were disqualified and removed from the ballots. When the ballots were counted, the PSL received only 10 percent of the votes and elected twenty-eight deputies, fourteen of whom were later disqualified and not allowed to take their seats. Cyrankiewicz of the Polish Socialist Party became prime minister. Stanisláw Mikolajczek, fearing for his life, fled back to the west.[173] So much for the promise of free and unfettered elections.

* * *

The refusal of the Polish foreign minister to consider the proposed Canadian compromise presented to him at the U.N. General Assembly in September 1947 was undoubtedly a reflection of the deteriorating state of international relations at that time. At about the same time, Dr. Fiderkiewicz left Ottawa and returned to Warsaw, where he was reported to be in line for a new post as the Polish ambassador to Hungary.[174] Perhaps Fiderkiewicz had not been forceful enough in dealing with the Canadian government with regard to the missing treasures. He had certainly failed to discover their where-abouts, let alone secure their return. Some months later a Canadian newspaper reported that he had resigned from the Polish diplomatic service and was apparently living in an Italian villa while he awaited the completion of arrangements to go to the United States, where he had worked before the Second World War.[175]

Once its compromise proposal had been rejected by the government of Poland, the Department of External Affairs began to look for alternative ways of solving its dilemma. It had already suggested that the Polish legation could take action in the Canadian courts against persons it believed had wrongfully disposed of Polish state property; alternatively, it could go to court to secure the recovery of such property once its wherabouts had been discovered.[176]

At this point the Department of External Affairs approached the Department of Justice to see whether the Royal Canadian Mounted Police could be employed to search for the missing Polish treasures. Louis St. Laurent wrote his Justice counterpart, J.R. Ilsley, that he was anxious to take steps to alleviate the rather strained relations between

Canada and the Republic of Poland. He asked the Justice minister to have the RCMP carry out a search for the missing treasures and he suggested that, once they had been found, the RCMP should keep them under surveillance until the Polish legation had decided what action it wished to take.

Ilsley agreed to St. Laurent's request, and that same day the police force assigned a senior non-commissioned officer to the task of locating the Polish treasures. His instructions laid out the parameters to be followed during the investigation. The treasures were to be treated as missing property, since there was no indication of criminal intent on the part of those in possession of the objects. Accordingly, no search warrant could be issued, nor could any demand for the property be made by the police once it had been located. If possible, however, surveillance over the items was to be maintained.[177]

It was the end of January before the RCMP met with any success. It had secured the name of the company that had moved the Polish treasures from Ste. Anne-de-Beaupré to Quebec City in 1946, and by following up on this lead, it was able to trace delivery to the convent of the Augustine Sisters who operated the Hôtel-Dieu Hospital in Quebec.[178] On January 29, 1948, Corporal Carrière and Constable Houle visited the convent to confirm what had been discovered. They were received by Mother St. Henri, the mother superior. Upon being assured that the treasures were indeed there, they asked to see them in order to verify how many trunks were in storage. Mother St. Henri was most cooperative. Later that day, when Constable Houle returned with Inspector Belec, the Officer Commanding the Quebec Sub-Division of the RCMP, Mother St. Henri assured the inspector that she would notify the mounted police before turning over the trunks to anyone.[179]

The next day Commissioner Wood of the RCMP notified the minister of Justice that the missing Polish treasures formerly housed in Ste. Anne-de-Beaupré had been discovered at the Hôtel-Dieu in Quebec City.[180] External Affairs does not seem to have been told of these developments until February 13 — two weeks later. Lester Pearson of External Affairs reported the discovery to Dr. Zygmunt Bielski at the Polish legation that same day, no doubt hoping that the legation would decide to pursue a legal remedy without delay.[181] The course of action the Polish legation decided upon, however, was not one the Department of External Affairs had expected. The Polish authorities decided to deal directly with the Augustine Sisters at the Hôtel-Dieu. The legation telephoned the mother superior of the convent on February 14 to inform the sisters that unless they surrendered the Polish property voluntarily, it would take legal action.[182] Dr. Bielski's next communication was a firmly worded letter to the convent, written on February 21, in which he asserted his wish to settle the affair of the Polish treasures without a confrontation — and without publicity that might prove distasteful to the Augustine Sisters and the Roman Catholic Church. Since he had not heard from her, however, he had now instructed his lawyers to take the necessary steps for the recovery of the treasures, and until such time as he personally retrieved them from the Hôtel-Dieu, the Augustine Sisters were to be held responsible for retaining possession of the objects in question. Bielski asked Mother St. Henri to acknowledge that she was prepared to accede to his request by four o'clock on the afternoon of February 25, 1948.[183]

Two days later, on the twenty-third, Dr. Wracláw Babinski of the London Poles issued a very formal communication to Mother St. Henri. Having just learned that certain unauthorized people were trying to take possession of the twenty-four cases he had deposited at the Hôtel-Dieu, he reminded Mother Superior that the contract of deposit between them was still valid and that he alone had the right to control the objects; no one else was entitled to claim possession of them from the Augustine Sisters. Accompanying this formal declaration was a personal letter to Mother St. Henri in which Babinski apologized to the sisters for any discomfort on their part for which he might be responsible. He thanked them for their help in storing the articles in question and concluded his letter with these words: "Pray for us, pray for our cause — Christian and Catholic, pray for me, my Reverend Mother."[184]

At this point, with two Polish factions each urging completely incompatible courses of action, Mother St. Henri probably wished that she had never heard of the Polish national treasures.

CHAPTER FOURTEEN
A Bird in the Bush

February 25, 1948, was to be a fateful day. That afternoon, Inspector R.J. Belec, the Officer Commanding the Quebec Sub-Division of the RCMP, received information from Maurice Boisvert, a barrister representing the Polish legation, that the Polish treasures had been removed from the Hôtel-Dieu.[185] Sergeant Allard and Constable Houle were immediately sent to speak to Mother St. Henri to determine what had happened. When they reached the convent at around 5:00 p.m., they were told that Mother Superior was occupied and could not see them. The two men therefore informed the sister at the entrance that they would return at 10:00 the next morning. At the appointed time Mother St. Henri came to speak to them. She told them that the cases in question were no longer at the convent. When Allard and Houle asked to see the storage area, Mother Superior replied that she could not let them into the cloister and suggested that their assignment at the Hôtel-Dieu should be finished since the treasures were no longer there. Asked when the cases had been removed, Mother St. Henri did not wish to reply and directed them to her lawyer, J.M. Guérard.[186] It looked as if the force's worst fears had been realized. Once again, the Polish national treasures had gone missing!

By the following day, February 27, Commissioner Wood of the RCMP reported these new developments to the minister of Justice, J.L. Ilsley. Wood stated that headquarters in Montreal had telephoned that morning to report that Quebec provincial authorities had assumed custody of the twenty-three trunks and one box containing the Polish treasures and that, consequently, the Hôtel-Dieu was no longer prepared to deal with the police on this matter. The RCMP had been keeping the hospital under surveillance, but delivery trucks were continually entering and leaving, and these could not be inspected since the police had no authority to search.[187] On March 2 Commissioner Wood again wrote Ilsley, this time to report that the Mounties were not certain that the treasures had been removed from the Hôtel-Dieu. In view of the refusal of the mother superior to let the police examine the storage area, it was possible that the treasures might still be on the premises.[188]

* * *

Rumours of political intrigue surrounding the Polish treasures had been circulating in Quebec City for several days, but it was not until Premier Maurice Duplessis issued a press release on March 3 that the general public received any official information. What people learned that day was astounding. Duplessis stated:

> Several chests of Polish art treasures, of a religious and historical as well as artistic value that cannot be estimated, had been given for safekeeping to the Reverend Sisters of the Hôtel-Dieu of Quebec because the authorities were afraid that they might be sabotaged or stolen by Stalin and his Communists.
>
> A short while ago, members of the Federal police, without search warrants and in an illegal manner, forced their entrance not only into the convent of the Sisters of the Hôtel-Dieu, but also into their cloister.
>
> In view of the incident, which caused much agitation and humiliation among the Sisters, and of a request to the Premier by the Sisters asking protection against such procedures and the violation of the cloister of the Reverend Sisters, we have decided that it was the duty of the Province of Quebec to intervene and stop any repetitions of incidents both regrettable and revolting to the population of our province.
>
> Stalin and his accomplices ... want to establish in Europe and throughout the world an atheist regime, a

Government without God that is deeply repugnant to the Province of Quebec.

We are much grieved that the Federal authorities of our country, particularly the Ministers representing the Province of Quebec in the country's Government, made themselves the collaborators of Stalin and his Polish Government to the point that they ordered their police to ignore the laws and to violate the cloister of that noble order.

The Government of the Province of Quebec could not in good conscience remain indifferent to this attack against our dearest traditions. The Government of the Province of Quebec has never been and will never be a collaborator of Stalin or of any of his satellite governments imposed by force, murder and the most ignoble and anti-democratic measures.

To protect the Reverend Sisters of the Hôtel-Dieu and our traditions against repetitions of such incidents, the Government of the Province of Quebec has seized and impounded these treasures and has placed them in the vaults of the Provincial Museum....

We will see that the prerogatives and traditions of the province, particularly our religious traditions, are respected by one and all.[189]

In the press release, the premier — who was clearly not pulling any punches — included the text of a letter written one week earlier by Mother St. Henri, thanking Duplessis for accepting the Polish treasures at the Provincial Museum. In her letter, Mother St. Henri stated:

It is unnecessary to explain to you the extreme embarrassment in which we found ourselves after the visit of the Mounted Police. From the founding of our convent this was certainly the first time that we had to deal with constables who demanded to visit our community, so that we found ourselves in a situation requiring us to accept with regret their entry into our cloister and to permit also the examination of the cases deposited with us.

These incidents were very difficult for us and we pray, God, that thanks to your intervention, we will in future be free of such troubles.[190]

Reaction to Premier Duplessis's press release was not long in coming. On that same day, March 3, Mother St. Henri issued a communiqué of her own, in which she explained that her religious community had accepted some months before a deposit of valuable objects from a Polish gentleman. In February another Polish citizen, the chargé d'affaires of the Republic of Poland, demanded that these cases be handed over to him. Learning of this, the man who had entrusted the objects to the sisters in the first place forbade them to deliver the cases to anyone but himself. He then ordered their removal to the Provincial Museum. At this point, Mother St. Henri asked the premier to transport the articles to the museum, where they could be properly housed and looked after. Duplessis agreed to the transfer, thus excusing the sisters from any involvement in a legal dispute over the ownership of the objects. Mother St. Henri insisted that there had been no seizure of the cases on the part of the provincial government. "We accepted a deposit and we surrendered it according to the instructions of the depositor," the Mother Superior concluded.[191]

Commissioner S.T. Wood of the Royal Canadian Mounted Police also issued a statement that same day, one that was obviously designed to answer the premier's accusations. First he reviewed the Justice minister's request that the RCMP determine the whereabouts of the Polish national treasures. Having been informed late in January that the articles in question were stored at the Hôtel-Dieu, Corporal Carrière and Constable Houle had been sent to the convent of the Soeurs Augustines on the twenty-ninth of that month to confirm this report. There they were received by Mother St. Henri. Commissioner Wood's report continues:

The Mother Superior, on learning the purpose of the visit, quite readily informed the members of the police that the treasures were still in the basement of the convent and offered to show them to the members. The offer was accepted and the room containing the treasures was visited by the two members of the police, accompanied by the Mother Superior and her assistant.

It was the Mother Superior who directed the police through the cloister, although in fact the police offered to proceed to the basement by an outside entrance.

The purpose of the interview was to seek information and the RCMP made no demand to enter, much less was there any suggestion that they had a right to search. They were received most courteously by the Mother Superior.

At a later date Inspector Rene J. Belec again interviewed the Mother Superior and was received in a most cooperative and understanding manner.

The police were fully aware that there was a dispute as to the rightful ownership or possession of the articles and the Commissioner of the police had specifically instructed that they should be treated as missing property and that no demand could be made to produce the property nor if located should any seizure action be taken.[192]

* * *

At this point there are two conflicting stories concerning the RCMP's January visit to the Hôtel-Dieu. Premier Duplessis, in his March 3 statement, alleged that the police had violated the cloister of the Augustine Sisters by forcing their way in. Later that same day, Commissioner Wood told a very different story, maintaining that the two policemen had entered the cloister at the invitation of the mother superior after offering to use another entrance that led directly to the basement storage area from the street. The commissioner described Mother St. Henri's attitude on this occasion as most cooperative.

In order to sort out these contradictory statements, it is important to remember that Quebec in 1948 was still a staunchly Catholic society. It does not seem possible that two French-speaking, Roman Catholic policemen in that era would have forced their way into the convent of a cloistered order of sisters. Such an action would have been at odds with their entire religious upbringing. It would also have violated their instructions for this particular assignment which insisted that the RCMP had no right to search. Accordingly when the police approached Mother St. Henri on January 29 to inquire about the Polish treasures, the encounter seems to have been an amicable one. She received them with respect, welcoming them and answering their questions. If the constables wished to verify that there were indeed twenty-three trunks and one wooden box on the premises, she was prepared to accompany them to the basement storage area where they could check numbers. The policemen, in their turn, did not ask to see the contents of the cases.

If one examines Mother St. Henri's statements carefully, one finds no reference to a violation of their cloister. In her letter asking for Premier Duplessis's assistance, she confined herself to an explanation of the dilemma in which the sisters found themselves with two Polish factions pressing them to surrender the treasures.[193] In her letter of thanks to the premier, which Duplessis quoted in his press release, St. Henri spoke of the extreme embarrassment and regret the sisters had felt after the visit of the mounted police.[194] This letter, however, was written a month after the incident took place. Of course the sisters were embarrassed by the situation in which they found themselves by the end of February, when they were being hard pressed by two opposing groups of Poles. That was not, however, their attitude when they were first visited by the RCMP one month earlier.

This leaves the actions of the premier of Quebec to be explained. Why would Duplessis exaggerate by labelling the RCMP's January 29 visit to the Hôtel-Dieu a violation of the Augustine Sisters' cloister? Why did he remove the Polish national treasures to the Provincial Museum? Duplessis was undoubtedly playing politics, a game which he played very adroitly.

CHAPTER FIFTEEN
The Premier of Quebec

The new player in the high stakes game of one-upmanship involving the Polish treasures had served as premier of the province of Quebec since August 1944. Maurice Duplessis's political career had begun in 1927, when he was elected to Quebec's legislative assembly as a Conservative representing the Trois-Rivières constituency where he lived and practised law.

To be a Conservative in Quebec in the 1920s was to occupy the political hinterland. The Conservative party had fared badly in that province for many years. The trouble began when a Tory government led by Prime Minister Sir John A. Macdonald condemned Louis Riel to death in 1885, after the French-speaking Métis leader's unsuccessful Saskatchewan rebellion of that year. French Canada was shocked at this treatment of one of their own. Then in 1917 another Conservative prime minister, Sir Robert Borden, introduced conscription for over-seas service. French-Canadians could see no reason why they should fight and die in the muddy fields of Europe to enhance the power and prestige of the British Empire. Against this background it had become extremely difficult for a Conservative to win a Quebec constituency. In fact, the Liberal party had been in office continuously in the province of Quebec for a record forty years when Premier Taschereau called the 1936 provincial election.

Maurice Duplessis was to break the Liberal stranglehold on the legislature. Working with a group of dissident Liberals, Duplessis formed a new party, the Union Nationale. Faced with charges of corruption and hobbled by the economic stress of the Depression years, the Liberal government went down to defeat in the 1936 election. The Union

Nationale formed a government and Duplessis became premier. Over the next six months he managed to outmanoeuvre his dissident Liberal allies and emerge as the unquestioned head of the Union Nationale party — "le chef," as he became known to his loyal followers. The political prowess of Maurice Duplessis was never in question thereafter.

Duplessis remained a conservative. The French-speaking inhabitants of Quebec had been involved in an ongoing struggle to maintain their identity ever since their land became a British territory in 1763. Loyalty to their traditions, their language and the Roman Catholic Church, which had played a major role in preserving this identity, had been essential to their survival. It was no accident that "Je me souviens" ("I remember") became the motto of the province of Quebec. Duplessis recognized the importance of conservative values — family, land, church — and milked these themes for all they were worth. A 1934 speech attacking the Taschereau Liberal government of that day has been reported as follows:

> [Under Taschereau t]here had been nothing for the farmer while flagrant privileges were handed out to foreign industrialists … no farm credit, no rural electrification program, insufficient assistance to the old parishes that were the backbone of Quebec. The land, the Church, the culture — all that was patriotic, godly, and traditional — was being jettisoned for urbanization, speculation, dehumanizing and mocking mammon. And among the teeming urban masses' self-reliant and prudent behaviour, the strengthening marrow of religious faith and practice, all that was dignified and desirable, gave way to frivolity, licentiousness, unruliness, alcoholism, and disrespect for God and state.[195]

Another favourite theme of Premier Duplessis was Quebec autonomy. Duplessis was not a separatist, but if he was going to defend the French-Canadian way of life, the federal government in Ottawa would serve as a convenient stalking horse. To fight for Quebec's rights was to rebel against assimilation. To fight for autonomy,

Duplessis claimed, represented not something new and radical, but rather a return to the real intent of the fathers of Confederation. It was an attack upon the bureaucracy and centralizing forces of the federal government that were constantly encroaching on the rights of the province of Quebec. Duplessis proclaimed himself to be both a conservative and a Quebec nationalist. He wished to bring together former Conservatives and Nationalists under the banner of the Union Nationale party.[196]

Developing a good relationship with the Roman Catholic Church was another essential part of the Duplessis program. This relationship was beneficial to both parties and, at the same time, meshed beautifully with the premier's conservative stance. It must be remembered that Quebec at mid-century was a very different province from the Quebec of today. In the 1940s the church operated the schools of Quebec, while sisters from Roman Catholic religious orders ran the province's hospitals, orphanages and homes for the aged. The Roman Catholic Church wielded great power in the province and affected the daily lives of all its Catholic parishioners. The Duplessis government was prepared to maintain and support these institutions, because without them the cost of operating the province's education and social services would have skyrocketed. With their backing in those areas assured, the premier was able to free up capital for roads, hospitals and schools while maintaining the lowest level of taxation in Canada, an attribute that would help attract foreign investment.[197] The relationship therefore worked well indeed for both parties.

Duplessis also developed an excellent working arrangement with the Quebec business community, which was at that time still predominantly English. His fiscal policies left these business leaders free to run their affairs with a minimum of government interference. Taxes were low, outside capital investment was welcome, international trade unions were discouraged, and the dissemination of socialist propaganda was outlawed.[198] In a letter to J.W. McConnell, the head of several Montreal businesses and the owner of the Montreal *Star* newspaper, Duplessis wrote:

> Communists should not and cannot be treated softly.
> The old saying, "Eternal vigilance is the price of liberty,"

is truer than ever, if possible. Communism is synony-
mous with atheism, disloyalty, and contagious poison
and accordingly, it should be treated as such.[199]

Sweet music, no doubt, to the ear of a business tycoon. Could
one find a more favourable economic environment in which to operate?
Could one build a more effective political combination than the
partnership between government, church and business that
Duplessis had assembled?

The arrival of the letter from Mother St. Henri of Hôtel-Dieu
requesting help in the matter of the Polish treasures proved to be a
stroke of luck for Duplessis. Intervening in the crisis gave him the
opportunity to pose as the deliverer of the harassed sisters of the Hôtel-
Dieu, as well as the staunch supporter and friend of the Roman Catholic
Church against the dreadful forces of international communism. He was
also further confirmed as the champion of Quebec's traditional values
and lifestyle. Above all, his involvement in the crisis gave him the
chance to tweak the noses of the Canadian federal politicians with
impunity. There was very little that the Canadian government could do
in this situation. The Polish artifacts were safely installed within the
walls of the Provincial Museum, well guarded by officers of the Quebec
Provincial Police. For Ottawa to send the RCMP to "liberate" the
Polish national treasures would be unthinkable. To engage in a lengthy
court action to achieve the same end would provide Premier Duplessis
with another example of federal interference that he would delight in
exploiting. Duplessis held all the trump cards. He was indeed a politician
to be reckoned with.

CHAPTER SIXTEEN
Political Manoeuvring

How had the actual removal of the Polish treasures from the Hôtel-Dieu been carried out? There was no public disclosure about this clandestine operation until 1961, when the last of the treasures were finally leaving Quebec City. At that time Walter Duchesnay, who had served for many years as Premier Duplessis's chauffeur and bodyguard, was interviewed concerning his involvement with the Polish treasures.

Duchesnay had been called into Duplessis's office on February 25, 1948, and was instructed by the premier to get the Polish treasures out of the Hôtel-Dieu before 4:00 p.m. — the deadline given to Mother St. Henri by Dr. Bielski, the chargé d'affaires of the Warsaw Polish government. Duchesnay counted on the fact that many vehicles moved in and out of the Hôtel-Dieu daily, bringing supplies for the hospital. He worked that day with eight constables from the Quebec Provincial Police. Their task was not an easy one: each case that needed to be moved weighed between 250 and 300 pounds, and twenty-four of these cases had to be shoved through a window in the convent's crypt and then pulled through four-foot-deep snowdrifts to a small alley where the moving vans waited. The plan worked well and the trucks moved out just before the deadline without arousing the suspicion of the RCMP, who were keeping watch over the hospital. The trucks then proceeded across the city to the Provincial Museum, on the edge of the Plains of Abraham. There they had to wait for several hours until the museum employees had finished their work for the day and departed. During the evening the cases were unloaded and taken to a vault in the basement, where they were to be stored under lock and key and guarded by two pairs of Quebec Provincial Police constables, each of whom worked a twelve-hour shift.[200]

The situation at the Provincial Museum in Quebec City after the arrival of the Polish treasures was ably described by a locally based reporter who visited the museum on March 4, the day after Duplessis's surprising disclosure of the removal of the Polish treasures. P.C. Dubois wrote:

> An armed guard of Provincial Police stands watch night and day at the Provincial Museum here, I found today on a visit to the massive grey stone building overlooking the historic Plains of Abraham....
>
> Visitors roam at will through the museum's departments on three floors during visiting hours. But two officers guard the door leading to the basement's steel vaults and 36 [sic] chests containing $1,000,000 in Polish art spirited into the building from a cloistered convent here in the night of February 25....
>
> Men on the night shift — which changed when the museum's doors closed at 5:00 p.m. — could be prompted into saying only that before the dispute over ownership of the treasures is finally settled, they'll know something about art. The long hours are spent looking over the works on view.
>
> The two men on the day shift would not even comment on whether or not they were at all interested in art. To all questions on the subject, they merely grinned good-naturedly or shook their heads.
>
> A woman employee of the museum since it was opened in 1933 was more cooperative.
>
> "I might as well tell you, for you'll read about it in the papers anyway," she said. "The Polish treasures — trunks and trunks of them — are in the vaults downstairs." ...
>
> As for the vaults — "Well, you should see them," she said. "But nowadays, not even the museum workers are permitted to enter them without the police tagging along."[201]

* * *

On that same day, the House of Commons met at three o'clock, and Louis St. Laurent, the secretary of state for External Affairs, made a statement that afternoon about the Polish art treasures. He denied categorically Duplessis's statement of the previous day that the RCMP had forced their entrance into the cloister of the Augustine Sisters at the Hôtel-Dieu, citing as evidence the statements of the RCMP commissioner and of Mother St. Henri. He described Duplessis's statement as a ridiculous attempt to smear the ministers who represented Quebec in the federal cabinet. Referring to the fact that the provincial government had seized and impounded the Polish treasures, St. Laurent said that this was exactly what the federal government had refused to do when asked. In Canada, the government did not seize objects to which there were disputing claimants; under such circumstances, according to St. Laurent, the claimants could resort to the Canadian courts for a judgement concerning their property if they wished. The Canadian government accorded to the Polish government the same consideration it would grant to any other government with respect to its property situated within Canada. He concluded by reminding the members of the House of Commons that the present government of Poland had for the past two years been the legal government of that country, recognized by most nations around the world.[202]

The premier of Quebec replied to St. Laurent's comments the next day, saying that he was not yet able to respond in full to St. Laurent's charges, but that he did wish to draw the public's attention to what he considered certain incontestable facts:

> The Right Honourable Louis St. Laurent is federal member for Quebec East. He is a citizen of Quebec City. He was Minister of Justice and he is Secretary of State for External Affairs in the Canadian Government. He should know that the Sisters of the Hôtel-Dieu in Quebec are a religious order appreciated to the highest degree and very greatly admired by the whole population of Quebec. He should know also that it is forbidden

under the most severe ecclesiastical punishments to violate the cloister of a Convent and that neither the Federal Government nor the provincial government may grant any permission to enter a cloister.

When it comes to relations between the Federal authorities and … the communist and atheistic government of Poland, one of Stalin's satellites, the Federal authorities deal with this government through an Ambassador and with all the protocol and respectful considerations attached to these diplomatic relations.

But when it comes to dealing with one of our noblest religious orders, Mr. St. Laurent and the Federal government use the Royal Canadian Mounted Police, the duty of which is to search for and arrest criminals under the jurisdiction of the Federal authorities.[203]

Duplessis's further, more detailed communication to the press appeared in the newspaper *L'Action Catholique* on March 10. Here he quoted from the letter Dr. Bielski of the Polish legation had sent Mother St. Henri on February 21, in which he stated that in order to trace the stolen Polish treasures and discover the identity of the guilty party, the government of Canada had placed the Royal Canadian Mounted Police at the disposal of the Polish legation. Duplessis objected strongly to the federal police force being placed at the service of the communist Polish regime. He repeated his accusations that the RCMP had annoyed, intimidated and humiliated the Augustine Sisters of the Hôtel-Dieu and, in particular, the mother superior — all because St. Laurent had himself enlisted the services of the Mounties to deal with this delicate matter. He suggested that St. Laurent could have communicated personally with the sisters of the Hôtel-Dieu instead of sending the federal police to harass them. Duplessis concluded by saying, "If Mr. St. Laurent is content with his conduct and his attitude on this subject, we are ourselves proud of our attitude and of the decisions we have taken. It is a question of principle. It is a question of character."[204]

After all the political mudslinging, the best summary of what had been happening appeared in an editorial in the March 13 issue of

Saturday Night, which commented that the peculiar and outstanding talents of Duplessis had seldom been better displayed. The situation was made to order for him: he could make faces at Poland from behind the shelter of the federal government, which was not in a situation to insult other nations lest it be taken to task on the international stage. St. Laurent was a minister of External Affairs; Duplessis was not. As long as St. Laurent and Prime Minister Mackenzie King continued to observe the amenities of international relations, Duplessis could accuse them of slavish prostration before communism. When they made inquiries about the whereabouts of property claimed by the present Polish government, he could accuse them of violating the sanctity of the cloister. Nothing could be better from the point of view of provincial politics.[205]

* * *

The first Polish treasures to be repatriated actually left Halifax on September 19, 1948, aboard the *Sobieski* in three boxes and two trunks. These were the articles that had been left behind at the Public Records Office in 1945, when the more valuable objects had been removed by Dr. Wracláw Babinski and his two curators. These historical artifacts had been released to Dr. Fiderkiewicz when he arrived in Canada in the spring of 1946. Included in the shipment were twelve Oriental and Polish carpets, four tapestries that were not part of the Sigismund Augustus collection that had decorated the walls of the Wawel Castle, and a Turkish banner taken during Jan Sobieski's Viennese campaign in 1683. Concerned that the Quebec government might attempt to seize this shipment as it passed through their jurisdiction, the Polish legation arranged with the Department of External Affairs for the customs inspection to be carried out in Ottawa. That way the containers could be sealed and shipped from the Canadian capital to Halifax in a sealed truck.[206]

News of the departure of the treasures via Halifax did cause a minor furore in Quebec. The Montreal press announced noisily that the Polish treasures were no longer in Quebec City, and rumours continued to circulate into the next day, until Duplessis finally invited the press gallery of the provincial legislature to visit the Provincial Museum and assess the situation for themselves.

Upon descending into the vaults of the museum, the reporters entered a large room containing the twenty-three large trunks and a long wooden case. The thick cement walls of the room and the doorway, which was closed by two steel doors secured by a combination lock, ensured the safety of the treasures. The reporter for *La Presse* was therefore able to assure his readers that the Polish treasures were indeed still present at the Provincial Museum and that they were well looked after.[207]

Travelling aboard the *Sobieski* along with this first shipment of Polish treasures were two key players in the drama that was being enacted in Ottawa. Both Swierz Zaleski and Zygmunt Bielski were on their way home.[208] Zaleski had served in Canada as curator of the treasures for eight years, first under the direction of the London government-in-exile and later as a public servant of the Warsaw government. Many changes had taken place in Poland since the curators had departed with their special cargo in September 1939, and Zaleski was about to discover how many.

Zygmunt Bielski, on the other hand, had only arrived in Canada with Fiderkiewicz in the spring of 1946. He had served as first secretary of the Polish legation and then, after Fiderkiewicz's departure, as chargé d'affaires until a new representative arrived from Warsaw. Dr. Bielski had worked tenaciously to secure the recovery of the Polish treasures. Unfortunately, he was returning with very little to show for his efforts.

CHAPTER SEVENTEEN
International Repercussions

In March of 1947 President Harry S. Truman, in a forceful declaration before the United States Congress, stated that the time had come for his nation to support any country resisting the advance of communism. This new policy was accompanied by requests for financial assistance for Greece and Turkey in their fight against communism. Later that spring the Marshall Plan offered help to any European nation struggling to get its economy back on a sound footing. A conference was held in Paris to arrange for economic cooperation among the participating states as well as to coordinate a list of requirements, but the Soviets — fearing American economic ambitions — refused to allow their eastern European satellite nations to participate.

In February 1948 the coalition government in Czechoslovakia, with its eleven non-communist members, was overthrown in a coup d'état. Newspapers hostile to the communist viewpoint were closed down, student street demonstrations were forcibly dispersed and many non-communist political leaders were arrested. President Benes was forced to accept a new cabinet with no anti-communist members, except for Jan Masaryk, the foreign minister, who had been a colleague of the president's before the war. On March 10 Masaryk's body was found lying on the ground below the window of his office at the foreign ministry, a bleak reminder of the seventeenth-century "defenestration of Prague" when two political dissidents of that era were removed from office by being tossed out of the nearest window.* Within two months

*The two dissidents of 1618 were Catholic deputy governors appointed by the Holy Roman Emperor to rule Bohemia, a strongly Protestant province at that time. The two governors were seized by a crowd of irate Protestants and

President Benes had also been forced to retire. News of these events in Czechoslovakia shook the western world, perhaps due in part to pangs of conscience arising out of the shabby way these same Czech statesmen had been treated at the time of the Munich deal with Hitler in September 1938.

Subsequently, the battle lines hardened. In April 1948 Congress finally approved the massive influx of cash that was needed to launch the Marshall Plan. At about the same time, Britain, France and the United States combined their zones of occupation in Germany and introduced a common currency to serve the whole area. The Russians retaliated in June by cutting off all access to West Berlin by road and by rail. Before the end of the month the British and Americans had organized the Berlin airlift, which kept the city's two and a half million inhabitants supplied with the food and fuel they needed to survive. Day and night for almost a year, Allied planes landed, at a rate of one a minute.

On April 4, 1949, the North Atlantic Treaty Organization was established. Twelve countries — Britain, France, Belgium, the Netherlands, Luxembourg, Norway, Denmark, Iceland, Italy, Portugal, Canada and the United States — promised to come to the aid of any fellow member in the event of an attack by an outside power and to coordinate military planning in order to carry out joint defensive operations effectively. One month later the Federal Republic of Germany, with its capital at Bonn, was formed out of the former British, French and American zones of occupation.

In Poland, the communist government was busy consolidating its authority over every aspect of national life. Immediately after the war the large estates of aristocrats were confiscated and the land redistributed among the peasants who had worked on the estates. By 1947, however, the peasants were being forced to band together on large collective farms. Eventually there were ten thousand such

---

thrown from a window of the Royal Palace in Prague Castle. The Protestant leaders proceeded to establish a revolutionary government in Prague and to expel the Roman Catholic Archbishop and the Jesuits from the city. Two Catholic armies were organized to invade Bohemia and, very shortly, the first battles of the Thirty Years War were under way. This conflict developed into a very bitter struggle which devastated Germany (1618-48).

Jozef Polkowski, Paris 1940.

Dr. Fiderkiewicz, the Warsaw Polish ambassador, holding Szczerbiec at the Bank of Montreal branch in Ottawa, November 7, 1946.

Probably November 1947.

Polkowski: "For memory of the greatest pike."

Polkowski at work at the delicatessen in Ottawa.

Premier Maurice Duplessis of Quebec.

Professors Marconi, Morelowski and Szablowski of Poland at
the Bank of Montreal branch in Ottawa, December 1958.

Crowd at the Wawel Castle waiting to view the first shipment of returning national treasures, February 1959.

The concert pianist Witold Malcuzynski takes a bow after a performance at the Wawel Castle to celebrate the return of the Polish treasures, February 1959.

Cartoon published in February 1961, depicting Professors Lorenz (of Warsaw) and Szablowski (Cracow) fighting for possession of the Flemish royal tapestries.

Jozef Polkowski visits Poland in April 1961.

farms, mostly in western Poland on land that been annexed from Germany. Those peasant farmers still holding private land were faced with compulsory quotas they had to deliver to the government at prices fixed by the regime. In June 1948 a new series of political trials began involving members of the Polish Peoples' Party, priests, and pre-war socialists. Editors of several Peoples' Party newspapers were arrested and imprisoned for as long as fifteen years. About that same time Wládysláw Gomulka was demoted from his position as deputy premier and general secretary of the Polish Workers' Party, the party Stalin had favoured at the time of the 1947 Polish election. Later, Gomulka and other political leaders who had fallen from favour were arrested and imprisoned. By 1949 the rights of the Roman Catholic Church were under attack. The church's lands were nationalized and its charitable institutions taken over by the state. Religious instruction in the schools was forbidden and chaplains were banned from prisons and hospitals. Then, in 1952, three bishops and several priests, who had been put on trial for spying for the United States, received sentences of execution or imprisonment. A year later the primate of the Polish church, Cardinal Wyszinski, was placed under house arrest.[209]

* * *

On November 6, 1948, Canadian Prime Minister William Lyon Mackenzie King retired. King had served for twenty-one and a half years, longer than any previous first minister in the British Commonwealth of Nations. He had guided Canada through the good years of the 1920s, part of the Depression, and then through the Second World War. A short, stout, greying individual, King had never been popular with the Canadian public. But he was an astute and gifted politician who succeeded in winning five elections — in 1921, 1926, 1935, 1940 and 1945. King has often been described, therefore, as the political leader Canadians disliked least. At the time of his retirement he was succeeded by Louis St. Laurent, which in turn left room for Lester Pearson to step into the position of secretary of state for External Affairs. These two men were to bear the burden of the ongoing dispute over Poland's national treasures.

* * *

The initial reaction in Poland to the news concerning their national treasures was remarkably low key. The Canadian chargé d'affaires in Warsaw, K.P. Kirkwood, visited the Polish Foreign Ministry on March 5 to discuss several matters of a general nature. The Polish officer who received Kirkwood that evening immediately asked him for further information about the startling news that had arrived from Quebec City. As Kirkwood had not had time to decode the latest messages from Ottawa before leaving the Canadian legation, he had no clear details to report. The Polish official reiterated the claim of his government that it was Canada's responsibility to retrieve his country's property which was being illegally detained in Canada and to restore it to its rightful owners.[210] Kirkwood remarked in a later dispatch that he was amazed at the silence of the Polish press on the subject of the Polish treasures. Perhaps the government of Poland, totally surprised by developments in Canada, was not prepared to orchestrate a response in the national press.

That changed in December. The first Polish publication to break the reign of silence was *Przekroj* ("Cross Cut"), a weekly photogravure magazine. An editorial writer, after attacking Canada in general and Duplessis in particular, went on to ask:

> Where is our guarantee that this Duplessis, who is untouchable and for whom the Canadian government accepts no responsibility, will not tomorrow open an antique shop on Fifth Avenue in association with Messrs. Babinski and Polkowski.... We must break our silence on the Wawel treasures. Let the whole world know how a cultured western country approaches the problem of the culture of other nations. This unbearable scandal must end at last.[211]

Soon every Warsaw paper seemed to have taken up the hue and cry. *Glos Ludu* ("The Voice of the People") reminded its readers that three years had passed since the end of the war. The Polish government did not maintain diplomatic relations with Quebec or Saskatchewan, the newspaper continued, but with the government of Canada. That was the reason why the suggestion that Poland should contest its case in a Canadian court against a Canadian province was so ludicrous.[212]

Commenting on the Polish viewpoint that a central government should have control over its constituent provinces, Kirkwood asserted that Polish officials consistently failed to understand the nature of a federal system of government. Their entire European background and training had been infused with the concept of a unitary state with an all-powerful central government. The concept of a federal system with state sovereignty in certain areas was quite alien to them. Probably very few Polish people had ever studied the historical evolution of such federal systems as those of the United States or Canada, wherein the central government was created by the states or provinces. Kirkwood continued that it was obviously very difficult for Poles to understand why the Canadian government could not demand unconditionally that the Quebec government surrender property placed temporarily under its control.[213]

Before long it was the turn of the Polish trade unions and students to voice their concerns. The central board of the Polish trade unions wrote to the Canadian Congress of Labour on December 14 asking for that organization's support in the effort to secure the return of the Polish national treasures.[214] The student protests took longer to coordinate and carry out; on February 16, 1949, eight hundred members of Poland's youth organizations met at Warsaw University to prepare a resolution to be delivered to the Canadian legation. The next afternoon four delegates — one woman and three men, all extremely well mannered and polite, arrived at the legation. The meeting was quiet and friendly, leaving Kirkwood with the feeling that the delegates were performing an assigned task without a great deal of zeal or enthusiasm.[215] Youth demonstrations occurred in other parts of Poland, but the similarity of the mass meetings and the uniformity of the resolutions passed led the chargé d'affaires to conclude that they were all officially sponsored and organized.[216]

In April 1949, the head of the Polish delegation to the United Nations broached the matter in a presentation to the General Assembly that was highly critical of the Canadian government. He

123

argued that because Canada had agreed to take Poland's national treasures for safekeeping, it was therefore responsible for their return. General Andrew McNaughton, the chairman of the Canadian delegation, replied that any examination of the issue in the General Assembly would be ill-timed and inappropriate. The Canadian government had received a communication from the Polish government on this topic just one week before, and his government needed time to consider this latest missive. McNaughton's objection seems to have effectively blocked further consideration of the problem during that particular meeting of the U.N. Assembly.[217]

Early in October, however, the Polish government returned to the attack, this time in the form of a booklet by Dr. Stanisláw Lorenz entitled *Canada Refuses to Return Polish Cultural Treasures*. Lorenz was an august member of the Polish academic community, a professor at the University of Warsaw and the Chief Director for Museums and for the Preservation of Historic Buildings and Works of Art. He presented the case for the return of the Polish national treasures in this way:

> We are already in the fifth year since the end of the war and in spite of the sustained efforts of the Polish Government, the Polish collections in Canada have still not been restored.
>
> This attitude of the Canadian Government, without precedent in international relations, offends all moral principles, and neither explanations nor evasions can circumvent the paradoxical fact that our cultural treasures entrusted to Canada for safekeeping, are still, four years after the end of the war, retained by Canada....
>
> The Polish nation demands that the priceless heirlooms of the past should be restored to the Wawel, that in the rooms of the Royal Castle there should hang once more the arrases with which they were adorned from the middle of the sixteenth century, and the priceless documents should be restored to the National Library in Warsaw.[218]

There followed a very well presented description of the many national treasures that had been sent out to Canada. Many of these artifacts were beautifully rendered in black and white photographs in Dr. Lorenz's booklet, which also included the latest communication from Warsaw to Ottawa. This memorandum, written on April 20, 1949, at the time of the U.N. General Assembly meeting, stated forcefully the Polish case for the immediate return of the treasures. The brochure concluded with a petition addressed to the cultural and intellectual workers of the world requesting their help in securing the return of Poland's historic relics which were being illegally detained in Canada. This petition was signed by the authorities of fifty-five Polish institutions — universities, colleges, academies, literary and historical societies and many more.[219]

Lorenz's booklet was distributed in October to the national delegations at the United Nations where the General Assembly was once again meeting. The Canadian legation in Warsaw reported that copies were also being distributed to all foreign missions in the Polish capital. About a month later Lester Pearson circulated a two-page memorandum to the heads of all delegations at the General Assembly reiterating the Canadian government's position with respect to the Polish treasures.[220] The war of words continued with a reply by the Polish delegation on December 1, 1949, requesting the criminal prosecution of those persons who were illegally holding the treasures.[221] There the impasse remained at the end of the year.

CHAPTER EIGHTEEN
Caretaking

W hen the Polish treasures being kept at the Hôtel-Dieu were removed to the Quebec Provincial Museum, there remained eight cases of artifacts that were unaccounted for. These were the cases that had been withdrawn from the Convent of the Precious Blood in May 1946, just after the arrival of Dr. Alfred Fiderkiewicz in Ottawa. Except for the black velvet robe of the Order of the Holy Ghost and the velvet hat from Pope Innocent XI, most of the artifacts stored in these trunks were military items — armour, shields and harnesses.[222] The Royal Canadian Mounted Police had not succeeded in tracking down any of the eight trunks.

Then, in December 1950, the Polish legation sent word to the External Affairs department that it thought the eight cases from the convent had been hidden in the village of Wilno in the Ottawa valley, about 75 kilometres southwest of Pembroke.[223] The RCMP sent two constables to investigate this report; they discovered that a new rectory had been built for St. Mary's Roman Catholic Church in Wilno approximately five years before. Included in the specifications for the new rectory were two large storage vaults in the basement, capable of holding a considerable amount of furniture, packing cases or boxes. Two similar vaults were also installed in the church proper at the same time. The rector of St. Mary's Church, Father Wilowski, was a very good friend of Dr. Wracláw Babinski, the wartime Polish representative in Ottawa, who frequently visited Wilno.[224] Although this information seemed to confirm the Polish legation's charges, External Affairs decided it would be impractical to pursue the Wilno lead until the Poles were prepared to take legal action to reclaim their property.[225]

In fact, the RCMP investigation of the Wilno site had come two years too late. The eight missing cases had been transferred to the Quebec Provincial Museum on November 15, 1948. In requesting permission to carry out this transfer, Dr. Babinski had explained his dilemma:

> We have still eight cases, well hidden in a secure location which has not been discovered by the reds. But, unfortunately, this hiding place is only temporary and I am obliged to move them in the next few weeks. Moreover the location presents some inconveniences from the point of view of conservation. It is rather damp.
>
> The idea occurred to us to solicit once again the proven kindness of the Premier and to entrust these eight trunks to the provincial authorities. As the cases in question are already in the vicinity of Hull, the plan which I suggest is to transport them to the provincial prison in Hull and to deposit them there, at least temporarily. Then, in due time, we can contemplate transferring them to the Provincial Museum. In any case the prison building in Hull is fireproof and offers advantages in other respects....
>
> The time is somewhat short as the transportation should take place before the cold of winter.... It is unnecessary to add that the strictest secrecy is an absolutely essential condition for success.[226]

Premier Maurice Duplessis's approval must not have been long in coming, as the eight trunks arrived at the museum in Quebec City one month later.[227]

* * *

Arrangements had already been established for the ongoing care and protection of all the Polish treasures at the Provincial Museum. The provincial government had agreed that time be set aside twice a year for the careful inspection and conservation of these priceless museum pieces by their Polish curator, Jozef Polkowski. In order to maintain proper security and to provide adequate working space for Polkowski's purposes, the museum would be closed during these semi-annual visits. Consequently, all the employees of the museum got two extra weeks' vacation every year thanks to the presence of the Polish treasures at their place of work.[228] The actual treasures were stored in metal vaults in a temperature-controlled basement room that had originally been designed for the safekeeping of the provincial archives. Walter Duchesnay — Duplessis's personal appointee as the guardian of the treasures — was the only person with the combination to the lock on the steel doors to this room. Once a week he entered the premises to check on the temperature and the ventilation. The Polish curators retained the keys to the chests and trunks containing the treasures.[229] Security was thus well safeguarded.

During Polkowski's first visit to the Provincial Museum in June 1948, each of the tapestries was taken out for inspection. They were unrolled on the marble floor of the museum's main hall where they could be carefully scrutinized, and there they were allowed to remain, fully extended, to air for twenty-four hours. Polkowski found that the arrases were in excellent condition. On that first occasion the curators only had three days to complete their work, but with the help of Inspector Duchesnay and of provincial archivist Antoine Roy, along with four policemen, the task was accomplished on time. Polkowski advised that this airing of the tapestries would need to be carried out every six months.[230]

When a serious moisture problem was discovered in the storage area a year or two later, the curators were able to cope with the problem. Fortunately, only one tapestry had been touched by mildew, but the steel swords and armour were covered with a film of rust, and the bronze articles and leather harnesses were mildewed. Polkowski and his assistant worked gamely to clean these objects but were not able to complete the process during that visit. On their return in the fall of that same year they found that moisture was still present in the storage area; they therefore requested that a ventilation system be installed in the vaults to remedy the situation. Duchesnay approached the premier and before the curators had departed the work was under way and one ventilator was already in place.[231]

The semi-annual trips to Quebec City for conservation purposes continued throughout the 1950s. By mid-decade the tapestries were being kept on a platform approximately three metres square which was raised about a metre off the floor of the vault. During the inspection they would be laid out individually on the floor in the great hall of the museum. There, each one was carefully checked and then left flat on the floor to regain its shape. After this process had been completed, the arrases were returned to the vault and positioned very carefully on the platform so that there was not the slightest crease in the fabric. The folds in the arrases were always on the outside of the platform so that they could hang loosely. In this way there was no pressure on the material in its place of bending.[232] And so the meticulous work of conserving the historic Polish artifacts went on year by year.

The only break in this routine occurred in the autumn of 1953, when the curators' entire visit was spent on an interesting exercise in publicity involving the well-known Ottawa photographer Yousuf Karsh. Karsh had made a name for himself during the war years with his portraits of famous personalities — Churchill, Roosevelt and de Gaulle, to name but a few. In the summer of 1953 Karsh had met Premier Duplessis while he was preparing a photo essay on Quebec City for *Maclean's* magazine. He suggested to the premier that it was unfortunate that so many beautiful masterpieces of art from Poland should lie on shelves in the Provincial Museum, completely inaccessible to the public. As a result of their conversation Duplessis agreed to allow Karsh to photograph items from the collection for a second *Maclean's* article to be published later in the year. It was the photography of Yousuf Karsh that occupied the attention of the entire entourage at the Provincial Museum, including the Polish conservators, between September 21 and September 25.[233]

The Polish Art Treasures: A Gift from Yousuf Karsh appeared in the Christmas issue of *Maclean's*. Karsh had prepared full-page illustrations of four of the Biblical tapestries from the Wawel Castle as well as photographs of such other items as Jan Sobieski's robe and hat of the Order of the Holy Ghost and the extraordinary armour with feathered wings worn by a Polish hussar. The text accompanying the pictures described the preparations that had been made to carry out the photographic assignment:

The coordinated help of many was required: free Polish representatives, Quebec provincial police, museum authorities, the Quebec film board, trusted electricians and discreet Quebec City merchants who would supply suitable background materials. It was September before everything was ready.

Karsh and his party were whisked from the Premier's office to the museum and admitted through a guarded rear door. Credentials were exchanged, keys were produced, and the heavy vault doors were swung open to reveal the stout cases in which the treasures lay.

Karsh admits that his heart skipped a beat as the cover was thrown back from the first chest. The armed police pressed close to see for the first time what they had been guarding for five years. Then Karsh and his crew, plus volunteer helpers went to work. For four days and nights with breaks for food and sleep, they performed the labour of art which resulted in these pictures....

To enable Karsh to do full justice to this and other tapestry masterpieces the Public Works Department of Quebec erected a great plywood wall, thirty feet by forty feet, and a system of grips and pulleys was devised to hang the tapestries without tacking or manhandling. For most of two nights Karsh worked on a movable platform under a battery of floodlights.[234]

Polkowski did not retain a very favourable impression of Yousuf Karsh. Initially, he had considered the Ottawa photographer to be an exceptional artist who was able to depict the historical artifacts in beautiful colours not always seen by the naked eye.[235] Later, however, Karsh's business dealings offended Polkowski's sensibilities. Polkowski reported that although Karsh had been very pleasant in Quebec City, he failed to keep a promise to meet in Ottawa after they had both returned to the capital. Karsh had told him of plans to publish the story of the treasures not only in *Maclean's* but in *Life* magazine as well. Polkowski, however, felt that Karsh had got these magazine contracts behind the backs of the Poles. There was no mention of financial remuneration for the Polish group, despite the fact that they had worked very hard in Quebec City. Moreover, since they controlled the keys to the chests, no photographs of the Polish treasures could have been obtained without their cooperation. As far as Polkowski was concerned, Karsh's only interest was to make money for himself.[236] In any case, the articles in *Maclean's* and *Life* duly appeared on North American newsstands in December 1953[237] and did much to raise the profile of the story of the Polish treasures across Canada and the United States.

* * *

During these post-war years, money was tight for those Poles who remained loyal to the government-in-exile in London. Throughout the war, subsidies from the Allies had enabled the Polish government to pay its staff in London and overseas. Once the western Allies withdrew their recognition in July of 1945, however, this financial support was gone as well, leaving the government-in-exile in dire straits. In order to alleviate the situation, the British government set up an Interim Committee for Polish Affairs with the authority to provide a measure of temporary financial support while the former Polish government adjusted to the new state of affairs.[238]

In Ottawa, the representatives of the London government-in-exile were also trying to come to grips with their new situation. Dr. Babinski, who had served as consul general for the London Poles, remained in Ottawa initially. He converted the former Polish legation into a boarding house to provide himself with some sort of income during this difficult transition period.[239] During the academic year of 1946–47 he was fortunate enough to teach at the University of Ottawa. Then, in 1948, he was able to obtain a teaching position at the University of Montreal — which worked out well for his family, since his wife and three children were already established in that city. In addition, he secured an appointment as an ethnic counsellor with the Catholic School Commission of Montreal.[240] Dr. Babinski credited his success in obtaining this position to the intervention of Premier Duplessis.[241] Still, despite these two appointments, Babinski wrote to Antoine Roy, the archivist of the province of Quebec, in November 1948, saying:

> My material situation becomes more and more diffi-
> cult.... From Ottawa it is evident that I can hope for
> nothing; I am reproached in certain circles for being too
> provincially minded — for having relationships with
> Quebec that are too close. I do not want to address the
> Premier of Quebec directly....Would it be too much to
> ask you to use your influence in my favour?[242]

Dr. Babinski might have considered himself hard done by, but there were others in worse circumstances. In August of 1945 Polkowski and Zaleski addressed a joint letter to Babinski expressing their concern over the ongoing conservation work on the tapestries and for the salaries they received for supervising the collection. They had been assured of their pay for September and October, but they were worried about the long-term financial outlook.[243] In October they wrote to two ministers of the government-in-exile expressing these concerns.[244] A month later a reply acknowledging the importance of their work came from Wiktor Podoski, the minister for American Affairs, who had been the Polish consul general in Ottawa from 1940 until 1944:

> The fate of both of you is more important than that of
> the officials of the Polish Foreign Office now in
> Canada.... You saved these treasures in invaded
> Poland and in invaded France. You preserved and
> looked after them.... Should your care for the collec-
> tion cease, the storing and preserving of these objects
> in dispersion with parish priests would give no guaran-
> tee of proper conservation. I consider it indispensible
> that the means of your existence should be granted....
> The officials of the Polish Foreign Office may become
> farmers, managers of boarding houses, lecturers, etc.
> Your task being not that of an office clerk, but of his-

torical and cultural importance, is still ongoing in the same scope and importance.[245]

Fine sentiments, beautifully expressed, but on January 26, 1946, the two curators received notice from the Interim Treasury Committee in London that their services would be terminated at the end of the month. They were to receive a gratuity of three months' salary as a measure of thanks.[246] In all fairness to Podoski, it should be noted that he had left London to return to Canada on December 25, 1945, and was no longer in a position to do anything for the two curators. Swierz Zaleski solved his financial problems by transferring his allegiance to Dr. Fiderkiewicz and the Warsaw government, thereby regaining his appointment as custodian of the Polish treasures at a respectable salary.[247] For Jozef Polkowski, still loyal to the London government, there was no such easy solution. Obtaining money for everyday living expenses proved a real challenge for him.

In 1945 Polkowski had been living at 29 First Avenue with Mr. and Mrs. Newlands for several years. He later wrote these words about the Newlands family and their concern for him at this time when his financial situation looked most precarious:

> Mr. Newlands was an Inspector of High Schools. I made my home with them for 15 years, until his death and later on until the death of his elder daughter. They were wonderful friends and most generous people. The old tale of Scottish stinginess is not true! Just to illustrate: when the British government ceased to recognize the Polish government in exile, I lost my job as custodian of the treasure and I lost my pay from London, England. After hearing this, I paid my rent. However, that same evening the daughter of my landlord returned the money, saying, "My father does not want any money from you. He feels quite indignant about the British government and is asking Mr. Polkowski to stay with us, not as a tenant, but as a friend." And so it was. I was touched to tears by their generosity.

> The house was a duplex and I stayed alone in one
> of them. They had a big garden and I looked after it.
> It was a very pleasant location, bordering on the
> Rideau Canal.[248]

This solved Polkowski's accommodation problem, but he still had to put food on the table. Unfortunately, he could not pursue his career as an architect because of language barriers and, even worse, because his eyesight was deteriorating.[249] As an alternative, Polkowski began to write dispatches for Polish newspapers in Britain. He asked not to have his byline appear over these articles because his family was still living in Poland.[250] Polkowski also sold Polish books as well as subscriptions to Polish newspapers,[251] but the income from such transactions would not be great. Moreover, for his twice-a-year trips to Quebec City, Polkowski received travel expenses but no actual payment for his conservation work.[252] As a result of all these circumstances, Polkowski's financial situation by the end of the 1940s was becoming extremely precarious.[253]

Eventually, in November 1951, Polkowski took a job as a night watchman at a hotel in Hull, across the river from Ottawa. His troubles were not quite over, however: a friend wrote to Babinski seeking help for Polkowski, who at that time was without a cent and could not afford to purchase the streetcar tickets he needed to get to his place of employment.[254] Dr. Babinski sent $75, which Polkowski said saved his life. In a letter of thanks, Polkowski described his new job thus:

> For ten days I have been working at the Hotel Chez
> Henri in the Hull area as a night watchman. My duties
> include winding up ten clocks which control the fire sys-
> tem and are placed in various levels of the hotel. Because
> of this, every half-hour I must climb 134 staircase steps
> and in the meantime put coal into boilers, clean them
> and take out the ashes, etc. Every night I put in about
> fifty to sixty buckets of coal through special doors called
> blowers, and once a week I need to clean the pipes in the
> boilers.... I start work at 12:00 at night and finish at 8:20

a.m. I get home about 9:00 a.m. and am so tired that I fall asleep in the tram. I usually sleep until 4:00 p.m. I cannot manage more because I have to dress and go out to buy something to eat before the shops shut. I get home, cook something and then get ready for work as I have to leave home at the latest by 11:00 p.m. to have time to get to work. I do not have any [free] Sundays or holidays. For this work I am to receive $100 a month.[255]

A considerable workload for a man of sixty-three. Understandably, Polkowski only stayed at this job for two months. By that time, he had also discovered that his employers were short-changing him on his salary — paying him only $85 a month instead of the agreed-upon $100; and no living allowance, although one had been promised.[256]

His next workplace was not much better. This time he was a cashier for a butcher in the Ottawa market. Polkowski described the shop as filthy and full of rats. On Fridays he worked from noon till 8:00 p.m. and on Saturdays from 8:00 a.m. till 8:00 p.m., dealing with about 450 customers on Friday and twice that number on Saturday. For twenty hours' work he received one pound of sausage and nine dollars, which just about covered his weekly expenses for food. His legs hurt so much after standing on bare concrete all day, however, that he found it difficult to walk to the streetcar stop to return home. On Sundays and Mondays he would sleep for twelve hours each, and it wasn't until Tuesday that he felt able to cope with life again — although he did remark in that same letter that he hoped to go to a friend's cottage from Sunday that week through to Wednesday.[257]

After a few months, Polkowski was able to change jobs again. This time he went to work at the European Delicatessen on Mosgrove Street, a newly opened business that belonged to one of his Polish friends. He worked there, at first for three days a week and later for a full six-day week, for at least a dozen years.[258]

Throughout all these years in Ottawa Polkowski remained a lover of the outdoors. He was a keen gardener and fisherman. A snapshot of Polkowski, standing on a dock holding a very large fish, has survived. On the back these words were inscribed: "To Mr. and

Mrs. Newlands for memory of greatest pike — J.P." [259] Perhaps it was the Newlandses who invited him to a cottage retreat in the Gatineau while he was working those very long hours in the market butcher shop. The son of a Polish friend remembers the curator of the Polish treasures as a frequent guest at their house, particularly on such special occasions as Christmas and Easter. He described Polkowski as a gentle, grandfatherly figure, an elderly man who often took him fishing.[260] Apparently, Jozef Polkowski was also very active in the Polish-Canadian Club of Ottawa. By organizing social activities for the members, he helped to attract to the club professional people who had come to Canada after the Second World War. His contribution to the organization was recognized when the Polish-Canadian Congress honoured him with a gold medal for his many years of service.[261] Life in Canada was not always easy for Polkowski, but it did bring with it many worthwhile moments.

* * *

Early in 1954 Polkowski learned that his wife, who had remained in Poland, was suffering from pernicious anemia. The situation was extremely serious, forcing her to lie perfectly still. She could not even take food unassisted. Polkowski arranged to send her vitamin B_{12} injections from a British pharmacy.[262] At this time he was still working at the butcher shop in the market. The working conditions were almost intolerable, but his income did enable him to send his wife the medicine she so desperately needed.[263] Despite these efforts, recovery proved impossible. The closest estimate of the date of Janina Urbanska Polkowska's death comes from a Canadian official who interviewed Jozef Polkowski in 1958 and reported that she had died three or four years earlier.[264]

This left Polkowski with only one close relative — a sister, Halina Grabowska, who was also living in Poland. She worked at the heritage site at Zelazowa Wola, about thirty miles west of Warsaw, where Frédéric Chopin had been born. Purchased by public subscription in 1929, Chopin's birthplace had been restored and made into a museum by the Warsaw-based Chopin Institute. The Polkowski family had a longstanding connection with Zelazowa Wola. Franciszek Krzywda Polkowski, Jozef's older brother and a landscape architect, had been responsible for designing a botanical park around the Chopin family home. His plan to landscape the site was approved in 1932 and work was completed five years later.[265] Franciszek Polkowski continued to supervise the park at Zelazowa Wola even after the war, when he served as a professor at the Warsaw Institute of Technology. He died suddenly at work in 1949.[266] Halina Grabowska continued to work at the restored Chopin residence as a clerk-administrator, dealing with members of the public who came to visit.

By 1956 Polkowski was himself very ill. He had no savings to tide him over a period of unemployment and no funds for medical treatment in this era before medicare had been established in Canada. When it became imperative that he undergo an operation to remove gallstones, his friends approached the Commission of the National Treasury (a Polish organization that worked throughout the western world to raise money for worthwhile Polish causes), which agreed to provide $500.[267] And so in September he spent sixteen days in hospital where the gall-stones were removed by means of a thirteen-inch incision across his abdomen. Upon his release from hospital, a Polish friend accepted him into his home to convalesce. His employer at the European Delicatessen promised to let him return to work for three days of work per week, and in the meantime he was able to draw $15 a week from the Unemployment Insurance Fund.[268] With help from his Polish friends, the crisis had been surmounted.

CHAPTER NINETEEN
Confrontation Again

During the 1950s the Polish campaign for the return of the historic treasures continued unabated. On March 25, 1952, the Polish ministry of Foreign Affairs sent a note to the Canadian government which read, in part:

> Seven years have elapsed since the end of the war. The Polish nation has already managed to rebuild many monuments of its history and culture. So far, however, the treasures handed over to the Canadian Government for safekeeping, in spite of numerous demands and protests on the part of the Polish Government, have not been returned to their rightful owner — to Poland....
>
> These treasures ... are being moved from one place to another, to different hiding places in monasteries, parsonages, farm buildings and stores, deprived of care and proper conservation indispensable for the preservation of these treasures for posterity, and are undergoing a gradual and inevitable process of deterioration.
>
> The Canadian Government has been finding ever new subterfuges in order to avoid the fulfillment of its obvious obligation of safeguarding and returning Polish property to the Polish Government....
>
> The Polish nation will never reconcile itself to the looting of its historic relics hidden by the Canadian Government and in these conditions doomed to ruin.

The Polish Government holds the Canadian
Government fully responsible for the state of the
Polish national relics and demands that the Canadian
Government immediately put an end to this injustice
and that it return these relics to the Polish State.[269]

The Polish academic community lent its voice to the campaign
for the return of the treasures. The professors of the Catholic
University of Lublin prepared an address to Canada's Catholic learned
men eliciting their support on this issue; a group of Warsaw University
professors made a similar appeal to their counterparts at the University
of Montreal and at Laval University near Quebec City. The faculty of
the Jagiellonian University in Cracow addressed a letter to the
Canadian minister of External Affairs requesting that the Wawel
treasures be restored to that ancient royal castle in Cracow as speedily
as possible. Their letter, signed by some fifty professors and lecturers,
was delivered by hand to the Canadian legation in Warsaw to be forwarded to Lester Pearson in Ottawa.[270]

* * *

Then, in 1954, a near disaster at the Provincial Museum in Quebec
added a new sense of urgency to the demand for the return of the Polish
treasures. When the vaults were opened for Polkowski's visit to the
museum in October 1954, the curators found patches of moisture on the
cement floor and water collecting in one corner of the room. The storage chests were moved, and mould was discovered on the floor — a
whitish growth like cotton wool. The walls and part of the ceiling were
damp, and in places the mortar was falling away. Polkowski was appalled
by what he saw. He reported the situation to Walter Duchesnay, his
Quebec counterpart, who arranged for an architect to survey the situation that same afternoon. The architect discovered that none of the
three ventilators in that part of the building was working. Cracks had
also developed between the stone slabs in the outside stairs above the
storage vaults, which would explain the presence of moisture in the
storage area. The blocked ventilators were cleared immediately, and

work was begun on a wooden floor raised on six-inch joists to ensure that air could circulate underneath. Before Polkowski left, tenders had been issued for repair work on the stone steps. One year later he was able to report that the walls were dry, the ventilators were working, and the outdoor stairs had been reset using lead to seal the joints between the stones — all this at considerable cost to the Quebec government.[271]

It was not long before these conservation problems in Quebec City became known in Poland. Stanisláw Mackiewicz, a former leader among the expatriate Poles in London, had returned to Poland, where he earned his living as a journalist under the pen name Cat. In December 1954 Cat Mackiewicz published excerpts from a number of Polkowski's semi-annual reports on the state of the treasures. These excerpts reported every difficulty encountered in carrying out the conservation work in Quebec City, from the time of Polkowski's first visit to the Provincial Museum in June 1948 to the very damaging report of October 1954. Polkowski's reports were, of course, confidential. They had been sent to Dr. Babinski, who in turn had forwarded them to his superiors in London.* Mackiewicz thus got his hands on these confidential reports, which he decided to publish, justifying his actions on the grounds of the condition of the Polish treasures which, in his opinion, could not survive further years spent in Canada.[272]

The ensuing comments in the Polish press concerning Mackiewicz's revelations were far more outspoken than any earlier criticisms. In an article entitled "Szczerbiec, the Coronation Sword of Polish Kings, in Captivity" the newspaper *Zycie Warszawy* expressed its views thus:

---

*At some time before March 1953 the Polish government-in-exile in London had split into two contending groups. Mackiewicz had served as the prime minister of the smaller of the two groups, sometimes referred to as the Château Group. The larger of the two — the Council of National Unity, or the executive group — was led by a Council of Three: General Anders, T. Arcuszewski and E. Raczynski.

This second group had the support of most Poles in Britain. The British Foreign Office dealt with them and advised the Canadian High Commission in London to do the same thing. (This information came from Michael Kulczyskowski, my London translator in July 2001, and from a memo from British Defence Liaison to External Affairs, dated June 28, 1956, found at NAC, RG 25, File # 837-40, Vol. 6769...8.2.)

Does the Canadian Government expect that, with time, the Polish people will forget where their national heritage is?

The Polish public remembers Canadian injustice. We thought of it particularly when our country, with all the cultural world, celebrated the hundredth anniversary of Chopin's death.... More than thirty original manuscripts and notes of the composer, as well as daguerreotypes of him, are becoming mouldy in the cellars of a museum in Quebec. We will never forget that the sword "Szczerbiec" grows rusty there, and many other national souvenirs are becoming spoiled. It cannot be expected that Polish patriotism does not suffer, knowing that, after so many years of apparent abandonment in a foreign country, the most cherished relics of her history are disintegrating — for example the "Holy Cross Sermons," the first attempts at sermons in the Polish language, more than six centuries old....

But Ottawa, following the style of life lived across the Atlantic and in the American comics, is not interested in documents in a foreign language. They may be spoiled, these Holy Cross Sermons or the Florian Psalter, since they are not appreciated by the Canadians.

The Polish public will never cease to demand the return of all her national treasures.[273]

With respect to the financing of the conservation work at the Quebec Provincial Museum, the same newspaper had this to say:

The financial propositions of Mr. Polkowski, the "custodian" of the collections, who had the function of a draftsman at the Wawel before the war and now is a salesman in a food shop in the province of Quebec, surely do not cause much trouble.... During the last eight years for the conservation of the treasures of a whole thousand years scarcely so much has been expended as would buy one sedan automobile. Net — three and one half thousand dollars! Is it possible to conserve more economically? For the conservation of the largest collection of tapestries in the world, for splendid collections of arms, staffs of hetmen, banners from the conquered,... the most varied souvenirs of the Middle Ages, accumulated in such a number never before seen in both Americas — Mr. Polkowski spends $1.20 daily!

It is easy to imagine how much Homeric laughter the conservation expenses of Mr. Polkowski would cause among the Polish historians of art if our most honourable national treasures were not involved.[274]

In order to keep these Polish newspaper allegations concerning the conservation process in perspective, Polkowski's comments on the subject are important. In writing to Dr. Babinski, Polkowski insisted the Polish press was quoting selectively from the documents he had written, taking passages out of context, thus giving an entirely different twist to the meaning he had intended to convey. The Polish newspapers reported every minor difficulty with respect to conservation, while mentioning none of the positive aspects of his reports.[275]

* * *

Nor was this the end of the situation. At the Wawel Castle in Cracow another piece of effective propaganda could be found. The authorities at the castle very effectively marked the absence of the celebrated Flemish tapestries from their walls by leaving large expanses of blank space, which were broken only by notices explaining why the tapestries were not there and where they had been sequestered. Since the castle hosted 500,000 visitors a year, the public was made well aware of the reason why the Wawel Castle had been deprived of its splendid collection of sixteenth-century tapestries and which country was to blame.[276]

CHAPTER TWENTY
Détente

Within a few months of the death of Jozef Stalin in 1953, signals emanating from Moscow indicated that the rigidity of the former leader's day was a thing of the past. Writers began to question certain orthodox communist doctrines. In Poland, a storm broke when a high-level Polish defector to the west began a series of broadcasts over Radio Free Europe about the Polish Security Service known as the UB. People were astounded to learn the extent to which Moscow had controlled every aspect of Polish life. In order to still the outcry, Wládysláw Gomulka, the nationalist Polish communist leader who had been arrested three years before, was quietly released from prison. In addition, the all-powerful head of the UB was dismissed.

In February 1956 Nikita Khrushchev denounced Stalin's rule at the Twentieth Congress of the Soviet Communist Party, opening the door for further change. When Poland's Central Party Committee met shortly thereafter, a program of liberalization was announced. Some 70,000 political prisoners were granted amnesty and released, while at the same time the minister of Public Security and several of the top UB officials were arrested. Then, in the summer, demonstrations by factory workers in Poznan led to serious confrontations with the police. The government sent in the army and the Poznan riots came to an end two days later.

When the Eighth Plenary Session of the Polish Communist Party met in Warsaw in October, Khrushchev flew in from Moscow unannounced. At the same time, Russian troops stationed in Poland were ordered to move toward Warsaw. In the face of these ominous developments, it was Wládysláw Gomulka who stepped in to avoid bloodshed. Gomulka convinced Khrushchev that he could control the situation, and the Soviet troops were promptly ordered back to their base. Two days into the plenary session Gomulka was appointed first secretary of the Polish Communist Party. In a speech to a huge rally in Warsaw he announced that Poland had started down a new road to socialism — a form of socialism with a human face. Before long, Cardinal Wyszynski was released from house arrest, and thereafter the Roman Catholic Church gradually resumed its normal activities. In the economic realm, 80 percent of all the Polish collective farms were dissolved spontaneously by the peasants who worked on them. As far as military affairs were concerned, the Poles asserted their national sovereignty by securing the removal of the Russian Marshall Rokossovsky from his position as commander of the Polish armed forces.

Despite these winds of change, Poland and the other Eastern Bloc countries were still ruled by one-party, totalitarian regimes. And so, when the people of Hungary in that same autumn of 1956 took to the streets to assert the right to control their own destiny, that exercise came to a bitter conclusion. At the beginning of November the Russian army, with the support of its communist bloc allies moved into Hungary to suppress this dangerous expression of free thought. Obviously, there were limits to dissent in communist eastern Europe. Gomulka made the same point in Poland during the election of 1957. He warned that crossing out the names of Communist party politicians in order to vote for independent candidates was tantamount to crossing out the independence of their country and erasing Poland from the map of Europe. Did Poles wish to be ruled by Gomulka and the Polish Communist party or by decrees issued in Moscow? Reforms they might have, but only those reforms that existed within the communist system.[277]

* * *

After Gomulka's accession to power, the views of Polish-Canadians toward their national treasures changed considerably. During the Stalinist era, most émigrés had opposed the idea of returning the treasures to a regime that did not, in their eyes, represent the Polish nation. Gomulka's government, however, looked like a far more independent one. Many expatriates thought that there was no longer any danger of the Polish treasures being seized by the Russians if they were returned to Poland. On the contrary, they argued that seeing the treasures back in the Wawel Castle might reinforce the Polish people's interest in their past and weaken their allegiance to communism.[278] Many Polish-Canadian newspapers, such as *Czas* ("The Times") in Winnipeg and Toronto's *Glos Polski* ("The Voice of the People") and *Zwiazkowiec* ("The Associate"), supported the return of the national treasures to Poland. The letters to the editor column in the latter paper contained submissions from across Canada supporting this viewpoint.[279] The trend was significant enough that even the External Affairs department in Ottawa noted a marked change in attitude on the part of the Polish émigré press.[280] Then, in October 1958, the Canadian Polish Congress, an umbrella organization representing about 150 non-communist Polish-Canadian societies, expressed the same point of view. At its fall meeting the congress passed a resolution favouring the repatriation of all their national treasures, provided that such a return could be managed so as not to be interpreted as an endorsement of the communist government of Poland.[281]

Meanwhile, in June 1957, Dr. Babinski died in Montreal at the age of seventy. The man who took over the chief responsibility for the Polish treasures in Canada was Adam Zurowski, an Ottawa businessman with a longstanding commitment to the London Polish government.[282] In the early months of the Second World War, Zurowski had served in France with the Polish army. After the fall of France he had escaped from the continent via Spain and Portugal to Gibraltar and England. From there he had been sent to Canada, where he became first secretary of the Polish legation in Ottawa, serving under both Wiktor Podoski and Wracláw Babinski. When the government-in-exile could no longer support its staff abroad financially, Zurowski established a successful insurance business on Sparks Street in Ottawa. Now he had been placed in charge of the Polish treasures. Changing times, changing personnel — perhaps a chance for a change in policy.

The other key player for the London Poles was, of course, Jozef Polkowski. In an attempt to win his support, various members of the Polish legation called on him from time to time during the 1950s. They offered to provide him with various publications from Poland should he be interested in receiving them, and of course they also inquired about the collection of national treasures. Polkowski ignored their advances. He did suggest, however, that these gentlemen should arrange for him to inspect the two trunks stored at the Bank of Montreal if they were really interested in the proper conservation of the collection. These trunks had not been opened since 1946, and Polkowski suggested that the artifacts be examined at the bank in the presence of a representative of the Polish legation. His proposals were always sidelined by numerous objections.[283]

After Polkowski's rather serious gallbladder operation in 1956, a representative called at his home on First Avenue to express the Polish legation's concern. Polkowski's recollection of the interview sheds a good deal of light on the relationship between the two Polish groups. He reported the visit in this way:

> I could not throw him out, so I asked him into the par-
> lour. I did not ask him to remove his coat or to sit
> down, so that while he was standing, I listened to his
> statements. He tried to be very civil. He said that the
> legation was sorry about my illness and wanted to help
> me. I declined the help and asked instead for someone
> with authority to go with me to the Bank of Montreal
> to do conservation work there. Once again, nothing
> came of this proposal.[284]

The evidence of strained relationships aside, Polkowski's concern for the historic artifacts stored in the Bank of Montreal seemed to be quite genuine. He visited the Quebec Provincial Museum twice a year and he was reasonably satisfied with the state of the Polish treasures located there. The trunks at the bank, however, were an entirely different matter. Since they had not been opened for years, no one had any idea of the condition of the invaluable manuscripts and other articles stored therein.

Jozef Polkowski received another most interesting visitor in the autumn of 1957. The person in question was Dr. Karol Estreicher, whom Polkowski had last seen in June 1940 when he had arrived in Aubusson with three suitcases of valuable historic objects to be evacuated from France. Estreicher, now a history professor at the Jagiellonian University in Cracow, was visiting Ottawa to give a lecture on Veit Stoss, the Nuremberg master craftsman who had carved the magnificent high altar in St. Mary's Church in Cracow.* He appeared unannounced at the delicatessen where Polkowski was working, greeted his compatriot very cordially, and suggested that Polkowski should visit him at his hotel. Later, when they were talking together in more relaxed surroundings, Estreicher asked about the Polish national treasures and speculated about their return to Poland. Polkowski, in his turn, raised the issue of gaining access to the trunks in the Bank of Montreal. Estreicher promised to pursue the matter when he returned to Poland.[285]

* * *

In the meantime, the Canadian government was considering its options. One member of the Department of External Affairs suggested that the best approach to the problem of the Polish treasures was to put the subject to bed until the alarm bells rang again.[286] This complacency would be difficult to sustain, however, in the face of advice submitted by the department's legal division, in whose opinion the Canadian government was responsible for the protection of the Polish treasures simply because they were the property of the Polish state and were located within Canada. This was a principle long established in international law. With respect to that part of the collection that had been accepted into the Provincial Museum under the control of the Quebec government, the Canadian government was indeed responsible for the recovery of these treasures from the museum.[287] According to international law the Canadian government bore the responsibility for the actions of all Canadian officials — federal, provincial and municipal — vis-à-vis a foreign government.[288]

These observations must have been rather disconcerting to the staff at External Affairs, especially since Premier Maurice Duplessis had

---

*"Wit Stowz" in Polish. The altar, a magnificent example of late Gothic art, occupied him for twelve years from 1477 until 1489. He stayed in Poland for several more years, fulfilling various other artistic commissions. Finally he returned to Nuremberg in 1496 and remained there until he died.

not altered his attitude to the Polish treasures one iota. In January 1956 during a debate in the provincial legislature the premier said:

> The treasures were confided to the government by Polish patriots and they shall never be returned to the Communist government of Warsaw. No deal, agreement or compromise will ever be made with the contemptible government of Poland for their return.[289]

Some time later Duplessis reiterated that neither threats nor promises would make him change his mind about the treasures.[290]

In view of the intransigence of the premier of Quebec, the Department of External Affairs decided to pursue the release of the two trunks at the Bank of Montreal. Most of the artifacts deposited there were uncontested Polish state property, according to an inventory prepared in 1946 by Jozef Polkowski.[291] In order to secure the release of this property, the consent of the two depositors would be required. Zaleski had returned to Poland in 1948 and had died there three years later. Since then, the Polish government had been trying to secure a release from Zaleski's heirs declaring that they had no right to any of the art objects in question.[292] Because Polkowski still remained loyal to the London Poles who had arranged the shipment of the treasures to Canada in 1940, gaining his consent to their release was likely to prove a great deal more difficult. In case Polkowski remained adamant, External Affairs approached the Bank of Montreal to determine under what conditions the bank might release the two trunks directly to the government. The bank replied that it would do this, provided the Canadian government agreed to indemnify the bank against any expenses that it might suffer as a result of such an action.[293] This was a substantial commitment, one the government was not prepared to undertake with any alacrity. And there the matter rested in the summer of 1957.

A federal election that same year brought about a change of government in Canada. After twenty-two years in office, the Liberal party was defeated and John Diefenbaker, the leader of the Progressive Conservatives, became prime minister. Sidney Smith, formerly the president of the University of Toronto, replaced Lester Pearson as External

Affairs minister. At this point the Polish legation in Ottawa might well have hoped for speedy action from the new government, but Diefenbaker indicated that his government was not prepared to move hastily. In view of the volatile nature of the question, the cabinet was planning to take a close look at all the implications before reaching a decision.[294]

Over the course of its investigation the External Affairs department interviewed both Jozef Polkowski and Adam Zurowski to ascertain whether there had been any change in their attitude concerning the fate of the Polish treasures. A.J. Pick talked first to Polkowski, whom he was meeting for the first time. He described Polkowski as a rather elderly, frail, well-dressed gentleman who possessed a quiet and dignified manner. Over the course of the interview Polkowski elaborated upon his concern for the treasures at the Bank of Montreal. All the metal objects were stored in one trunk, Polkowski reported, and should not pose a problem. However, he felt that at times the bank vault would be too hot and too dry for the books and manuscripts in the second trunk. There was also the possibility that vermin could get into the papers, particularly the parchments, which could prove an even worse disaster. When asked about the possibility of returning the treasures to Poland, Polkowski replied that he had solemnly undertaken not to release the treasures from the bank without authorization from those who had placed them there initially. He stated that he was merely a custodian or agent and he suggested that Pick speak to Zurowski, who had the responsibility of supervising the Polish treasures.[295]

Pick interviewed Zurowski three days later. He soon made it clear that he was not much impressed by the changes that had taken place in Poland under Gomulka. Zurowski then went on to indicate that he did not favour the immediate return of the treasures to Poland, because it was his belief that the treasures would not be well looked after in Poland. He supported this view by referring to complaints from Polish academics that neither the National Library in Warsaw nor the valuable library of ancient books in Cracow received sufficient funding to look after their collections properly. In Warsaw, for example, the books of the National Library were housed in five or six different places, many of them stacked in piles on cellar floors and staircases for lack of adequate shelving space. Zurowski did argue quite forcefully that Polkowski should be allowed access to the books and manuscripts in the Bank of Montreal for conservation purposes.[296] Perhaps their concern about the well-being of the Polish treasures might one day lead these two Polish gentlemen to decide that these historic artifacts would be better off on public display in Poland than mouldering away in an inaccessible Ottawa bank vault, but they had not reached that conclusion yet.

In the meantime, the following exchange of views amongst Canadian politicians took place at a meeting of the House of Commons Standing Committee on External Affairs on August 4, 1958.

A Mr. Mandziuk had just completed a short presentation arguing that the national treasures of Poland should be returned to that country.

> MR. SMITH (MINISTER OF EXTERNAL AFFAIRS): Mr. Chairman, these treasures are not in the custody of the Canadian government. Let us start with that statement.
> MR. PEARSON (FORMER MINISTER OF EXTERNAL AFFAIRS): That is true!
> MR. MANDZIUK: I was thinking of the particular rights to these treasures.
> MR. SMITH: I have struggled over this question, but I am now clear. I am bound — I say this with a smile — to accept the view of the Hon. Mr. St. Laurent (the former Liberal prime minister).
> MR. PEARSON: The minister is not bound to accept that.
> MR. HERRIDGE: You mean that you are delighted to?
> MR. SMITH: I am not. I wish we could legally return these treasures to Poland.[297]

Was it possible, in view of all these developments in Canada and beyond, that a breakthrough on the issue of the Polish treasures might be forthcoming?

CHAPTER TWENTY-ONE
A Musical Interlude

In eastern Europe, the bleak intransigence of the Stalinist era was a thing of the past. In Canada, there had been a change of government. It seemed as though some sort of compromise might be devised to break the deadlock that had left the Polish treasures stranded on Canadian soil for close to fifteen years. The key to the situation was the attitude of the London Poles and their representatives in Canada, Adam Zurowski and Jozef Polkowski. These men had been responsible for moving the national treasures to the Bank of Montreal in Ottawa and the Provincial Museum in Quebec City, and the historic artifacts could not be returned to Poland without their cooperation.

What was needed at this particular moment was a catalyst — someone who could initiate a dialogue between two opposing groups of Poles who had refused for years to even recognize each other's existence. The concert pianist Witold Malcuzynski would prove to be that catalyst.

Malcuzynski had been born in Warsaw in the year 1914. He had studied music at the Warsaw Conservatory and then under Ignace Paderewski in Switzerland. In 1937 he placed third in the Chopin International Piano Competition, where he met Colette Gavreau, another competitor. They were married the following year in France, where Malcuzynski made his international debut in 1940. After the fall of France he spent the rest of the war years in Portugal and Latin America. In the post-war era Malcuzynski was building an international reputation through concerts with famous conductors in America and Europe, in which he performed the repertoire of the Romantic era and, in particular, the compositions of Frédéric Chopin. In 1958 he broke his self-imposed exile from his homeland and returned to perform in Poland, where he was very warmly welcomed.[298]

The concerts Malcuzynski performed, both in the west and behind the Iron Curtain, brought him into contact with prominent figures from both sides of the political divide. In Poland he met the leaders of the academic and artistic communities as well as the politicians of the day. In London he was acquainted with the members of the wartime government-in-exile who had dispatched the national treasures to Canada in the first place. In Ottawa he was able to talk to the representatives of the London Poles as well as to the official delegates of the Polish legation. If anyone could bridge the gap between east and west, between the communist and the non-communist worlds, it was Malcuzynski, a musician who was respected by both sides and had no political axe to grind. Unfortunately, this kind of subtle manoeuvring cannot be easily traced. For obvious reasons, there is no record of key conversations that took place discreetly during Malcuzynski's concert tours.

At any rate, in the fall of 1958 Polkowski received a phone call at the delicatessen from another Polish gentleman, a Mr. Wiecko. He said that although Polkowski did not know him, he knew Polkowski, and he would like to talk about various matters of mutual interest. They agreed to meet the next day at the Honey Dew restaurant on Bank Street.* Wiecko arrived promptly and introduced himself as a consul at the Polish legation. In Warsaw he had worked as a professor at the High School of Agriculture and had also served as a member of the Polish Academy of Sciences. Polkowski found Wiecko to be a highly cultured, sympathetic person to whom he could talk quite openly. Their conversation ultimately involved the return of the national treasures to Poland. When Polkowski raised the question of conservation work on the articles stored at the Bank of Montreal, Wiecko explained that problems had arisen in Poland, where the government was trying to reach an agreement with Zaleski's heirs as to the ownership of the two trunks at the bank. The two men parted amicably with an agreement to meet again if any new developments

---

*Honey Dew was a chain of fast-service restaurants, similar to McDonald's or Tim Hortons today.

transpired. This was indeed an encounter on terms far different from the earlier meetings between Polkowski and members of the Polish legation.

Shortly thereafter Polkowski received another telephone call, this time from Malcuzynski, who was staying at the Château Laurier Hotel. Since he had met the pianist several times in Montreal at the Babinskis', he was not surprised at the suggestion of a meeting. The two men had dinner together at the hotel. During the evening they talked about the Polish treasures, and Malcuzynski asked whether the contents of the two trunks at the Bank of Montreal might be better off in Poland, where conservation measures could be undertaken. Polkowski agreed that the most sensible solution would be to return the artifacts to Poland. He felt that the concerns that had led to the hiding of the treasures years before were no longer valid, given the changing conditions in the world and in Poland. Malcuzynski told Polkowski that he was soon going to Poland for a series of concerts and that he would try to discuss the matter with the appropriate authorities there.

Then Polkowski heard again from Wielko, who reported that the testamentary problems with regard to Zaleski's signature at the Bank of Montreal had been resolved. He hoped that a Polish delegation would visit Ottawa before long with the necessary authority to open the trunks and examine the artifacts therein. Wiecko then asked Polkowski whether he would agree to the return of the articles to Poland if this were deemed necessary for conservation purposes. Polkowski replied that he would support their return because he was very worried that the ancient books and manuscripts might be irreparably damaged if they were left any longer without care.[299]

When Polkowski reported these meetings to Adam Zurowski and indicated his own support for the return of the treasures, he found that Zurowski had modified his viewpoint considerably. He indicated that he fully understood Polkowski's views and that he would support the return of the treasures to Poland rather than risk their possible damage by leaving them in the Ottawa bank vault indefinitely.[300]

* * *

Late in November 1958 the Department of External Affairs received its first indication that a breakthrough in negotiations had been achieved. On the twenty-fifth of that month the Canadian legation in Warsaw sent a telegram to External Affairs requesting visas for a small delegation of Polish scholars. These gentlemen were planning to visit Ottawa around December 3 to inspect the Polish treasures at the Bank of Montreal.[301] Within three days the required visas were duly authorized by the Department of Citizenship and Immigration.[302] Then, early in December, the Polish delegation arrived: Dr. Jerzy Szablowski, director of the State Art Collection at the Wawel Museum; Dr. Zbigniew Drzewiecki, professor of the Higher Music Schools, Warsaw, and president of the Chopin Society; Dr. Bohdan Marconi, chief conservator of historical artifacts; Dr. Marian Morelowski, professor of Art, Wraclàw University.* All four were well known to Polish-Canadians as men of distinction in their professions. None of them had been Communist party members.[303]

The delegation began negotiations with officials from the Bank of Montreal and with Adam Zurowski and Jozef Polkowski in order to make arrangements for the inspection of the two trunks. The hidden agenda, about which everyone was aware and no one talked openly, was the return of the two trunks to Poland. The assumption was that this would occur if it was discovered that conservation work was needed that could not be properly accomplished in the vault at the Bank of Montreal.

Before considering any release of the treasures, the bank insisted upon a guarantee that it would not be held responsible for any loss or damage to the treasures while they had been kept in its vaults. A document was eventually drafted that satisfied the bank's legal advisers and which Mr. Sieradzki, the chief consul at the Polish legation, was prepared to sign.

---

*Dr. Morelowski had served on the commission established in 1922 to oversee the return of Polish historic artifacts from the Soviet Union. Under the terms of the Treaty of Riga signed in that year, the U.S.S.R. had agreed to the repatriation of these objects. Dr. Morelowski was therefore involved in securing the return of the fifteenth-century Flemish tapestries to the Wawel Castle in 1922 — the very tapestries that were now in the Provincial Museum at Quebec City.

Zurowski and Polkowski, in their turn, were every bit as demanding. They wished to be present at the opening of the trunks; they wanted to have the opportunity to have the artifacts photographed if they were indeed being removed to Poland; and they were concerned about the wording of any press release in the event of such a return. They wanted any announcement to make it clear that the treasures were being released to the delegation as representatives of the Polish people, not to the communist government of Poland.[304]

When the Warsaw delegation began its discussions with the representatives of the London Poles, it was Jozef Polkowski who was first approached. Dr. Morelowski, who had known Polkowski in the 1920s when they both had worked at the Wawel Museum, telephoned him and arranged to have Polkowski meet him at the Lord Elgin Hotel, where he was staying. Dr. Szablowski, whom Polkowski also knew from his pre-war years at the Wawel, joined them there. These two men were probably chosen to serve on the Polish delegation, at least in part, because they would be able to approach an old acquaintance like Polkowski on easy terms. They arranged to meet again the next day, a gathering to which Adam Zurowski was also invited. Other meetings followed, but progress proved slow, the wording of any announcement to the press proving to be a real sticking point.[305]

Fortunately, Witold Malcuzynski had arrived in Ottawa, where he continued to act as mediator while the delicate discussions proceeded. In order to do so, he had been forced to cancel part of his latest concert tour.[306] Malcuzynski and his wife were virtually sequestered at the Château Laurier during these negotiations; they never went out, and Malcuzynski very discreetly saw those people he needed to contact.[307] He was kept very busy meeting with officials from the Bank of Montreal, members of the Polish legation, the delegates from Warsaw, and Zurowski and Polkowski.[308] Finally, he induced the Polish legation to accept the concept that the Polish treasures would be returned to the people of Poland rather than to the Polish government. In return, Zurowski and Polkowski agreed that the seals of the Polish government should be placed on the two trunks for the projected voyage back to Poland. The representatives of the London Poles were to be allowed forty-eight hours to photograph the treasures before the trunks were sealed.[309] And so, by December 17, Polkowski signed a declaration that he would agree to the transfer of the treasures from the Bank of Montreal to Dr. Szablowski if they needed conservation work that could not be carried out in Canada. Zurowski made it clear that he approved this declaration. Furthermore, he spoke of the visiting Polish professors with great respect and indicated his gratitude for Malcuzynski's mediation during the discussions.[310]

Approval for these arrangements still had to be secured from the two factions of the London government-in-exile before matters could proceed. Once contacted, General Anders' executive group telegraphed its agreement almost immediately.[311] Zurowski received no immediate reply from the Château Group, the smaller of the two Polish groups in London. Their representative in Montreal, however, did agree in a conversation with Polkowski to the return of the treasures. With this support in hand, Zurowski and Polkowski agreed that the trunks could indeed be opened, thus ending three weeks of difficult negotiations.[312]

* * *

By now it was two days before Christmas. The two trunks were opened at the Bank of Montreal on the morning of December 23 in the presence of the four Polish delegates from Warsaw as well as Polkowski, Zurowski and, representing the interests of the London Poles, Stefan Kontski. (Kontski was an artist who had served as a conservator at the Polish Army Museum in Scotland. Because of this experience, he had been chosen to work with Polkowski on his semi-annual visit to the Provincial Museum in Quebec for conservation purposes.) Also present were Dr. Don Norman (an American expert on Gutenberg Bibles), Witold Malcuzynski, and three representatives from the Bank of Montreal. Because this occasion was arranged by private individuals, no representatives of the Canadian or Polish governments attended.

As each of the two trunks was opened, Szablowski and Polkowski checked the contents against their inventory lists. Then Polkowski and Marconi carefully examined each object, and a new inventory was prepared, with comments on the current state of the artifacts. This new list matched, item by item, the inventories drawn up years before. Drzewiecki and Malcuzynski examined the original Chopin manuscripts, while Dr. Norman investigated the Gutenberg Bible, the only copy that he had ever seen with two volumes intact in their original bindings. This process took two days to complete. On the first day they worked until midafternoon, when they had to seal the trunks and return them to the vault because closing time at the bank was fast approaching. On the second day they finished their investigation by 2:00 p.m.

The men examining the contents of the two trunks did not find any catastrophic damage. Leather book bindings and the parchment used in the medieval manuscripts had dried out due to the aridness within the vault during the winter months, while insects had damaged some of the manuscripts, although happily only to a limited degree. The dry conditions had also loosened the metalwork on the casings and handles of the broadswords, and there was increased cracking on ivory items for the same reason. As a result of these findings, those present agreed to issue a joint declaration at the conclusion of their investigation. This protocol stated that many of the objects they had examined needed immediate attention, and that continued storage at the Bank of Montreal under existing conditions could only be considered dangerously negligent since it would undoubtedly lead to further deterioration.[313] These were strong words that paved the way for the removal of the historic artifacts and their ultimate return to Poland.

During this same time period the photographing of the Polish treasures from the Bank of Montreal was undertaken by Malak Karsh, with McDougall Microfilms of Ottawa taking detailed photographs of the most important medieval chronicles and Chopin manuscripts.[314] Karsh spent a couple of days at the bank, bringing the studio lights and background fabrics necessary for the operation. He recalled that there were guards all around watching his every move. Another visitor also remembered this photographic episode well:

> Zurowski's son, Alfred, ... remembers helping out at his dad's insurance office on Sparks Street one day when the telephone rang. His father asked him to come to the bank to witness something special.

> In the basement of the grand building, he recalls see-
> ing Szczerbiec [the notched sword] being handled and
> many other items being placed on a table draped with
> a cloth, to be photographed.
>
> "The sword is like a mythical thing with the Poles,"
> says Alfred Zurowski. "It supposedly got the nicks from
> banging on a fortified door in a fight with the
> Russians."[315]

On January 9, 1959, the Bank of Montreal formally released the two steamer trunks to Dr. Szablowski. Documents absolving the bank and Polkowski from any responsibility for the trunks or their contents had been duly prepared and signed the previous day. Dr. Szablowski, in his turn, promised to deliver the articles in question to the public and ecclesiastical institutions, or to the private owners to whom they belonged, as well as to pay for their transfer to Poland.[316] In the evening, after the paperwork had been completed, the Polish legation held a reception to celebrate the occasion. Zurowski and Polkowski did not attend, but Sidney Smith, the Canadian minister of External Affairs, was present and he expressed his pleasure at this happy out-come to the longstanding controversy.[317]

It took another ten days for shipping arrangements to be complet-ed. The two trunks were then moved to Union Station in a security van under an RCMP escort. From Ottawa, the trunks were to be transported on a special coach to New York via Toronto, Fort Erie and Buffalo. It was reported that the Polish legation decided to ship their artifacts by this roundabout route instead of using the Montreal–New York rail line because it did not to wish to risk any involvement with the Duplessis government by passing through the province of Quebec.[318] In Toronto the coach was switched over to the New York train. The RCMP con-tinued to guard the Polish treasures until the train reached Buffalo, New York, where the train was boarded by American officials who would ensure the security of the shipment for the remainder of the journey.[319] On the night of January 19 the train reached New York (see Map VIII — North America). There, city police and security agents saw the two trunks safely unloaded and transported to the seat of the Polish delegation to the U.N.[320] Two days later, they left New York aboard a Swedish vessel, the *Stockholm*, which was bound for Europe.

* * *

The voyage across the North Atlantic seems to have gone well. On January 28 Dr. Jerzy Szablowski sent the following telegram from the *Stockholm*:

> The ship having aboard the national treasures passes near the north coast of Scotland. The weather is sunny, the Atlantic Ocean is calm, direction Copenhagen via Bremerhaven, Goteborg.[321]

Upon reaching Copenhagen, the trunks containing the Polish treasures were unloaded and placed in a sealed freight car to travel by rail through East Germany to Poland.[322] They arrived in Warsaw on February 3, and the train was met by Mr. T. Galinski, the Polish vice minister of Culture and Art.[323]

The return of a part of their national heritage was greeted with much enthusiasm by the Polish people. An article in *Trybuna Ludu*, written when news of the return first broke in Poland, described the public's reaction:

> The information concerning the prospective return of a part of the Wawel treasures to Poland from Canada raised feelings of joy and satisfaction throughout the country. In many cities on that 10th of January all the newspapers which brought the first news were sold out rapidly so that about 9:00 a.m. there were no more dailies in the newspaper stands. The information concerning the treasures was this day the main subject of interest of the majority of the people.[324]

An exhibition of the Polish treasures was quickly organized and opened at the National Museum in Warsaw on February 7. In front of the museum building that day, national flags fluttered in the wind, looking especially brilliant in the winter sun. Long before the opening hour the entrance hall of the museum was filled with guests who had arrived for the ceremony — government ministers; members of the scientific and cultural community; the distinguished pianist, Witold Malcuzynski, and his wife; the Polish chargé d'affaires from Ottawa, Mr. Sieradzki; and the heads of foreign diplomatic missions accredited to Poland, including the Canadian chargé d'affaires. The director of the National Museum, Professor Stanisláw Lorenz, greeted the guests, expressing his joy at the return of the treasures.[325] (Zurowski and Polkowski refused to have anything to do with Lorenz, who had produced the very critical pamphlet *Canada Refuses to Return Polish Cultural Treasures*, which had circulated at the U.N. in 1949. This probably explains why he was not asked to be part of the Polish delegation that had visited Ottawa.) Before the exhibition closed five days later, 80,654 visitors had arrived to see these historic artifacts — more than 16,000 per day.[326] These numbers certainly speak for the enthusiasm with which the Polish people greeted their national treasures.

From Warsaw, the Polish treasures were sent to Cracow, where the whole saga had begun almost twenty years before. There they were to be displayed at the Wawel Castle. The exhibition opened on the evening of February 16 with a special concert by Malcuzynski in the Senate chamber of the Castle — a concert of Chopin's music. This gala event was attended by rectors of universities and museum directors from across Poland as well as by the regular workers at the Wawel Museum. Malcuzynski was given a gold medal by the city of Cracow in recognition of the key role he had played in the negotiations that brought the Wawel treasures home again.[327]

CHAPTER TWENTY-TWO
The End of the Affair

When the members of the Polish delegation returned home in February 1959, they took with them a personal commission from Jozef Polkowski. His sister, Halina Grabowska, who worked at the Chopin Museum at Zelazowa Wola, had been dismissed from her job. Because the post had entitled her to living accommodation on the museum premises, this was a double blow. Consequently, Polkowski had asked the members of the Warsaw delegation to find out whether anything could be done to alleviate his sister's situation.

Dr. Jerzy Szablowski replied in May 1959 that he had spoken to various people about Mrs. Grabowska and he thought that all should go well. In the same letter he commented on the possibility of Polkowski visiting Poland, saying that the invitation was still open. Dr. Marian Morelowski, in his turn, sent two telegrams to Polkowski. He indicated that he had intervened in Warsaw and that Grabowska's pension would be raised from 800 to 1,000 zlotys. In addition, she would be allowed to retain her place of residence at the Chopin Museum.

Drzewiecki was the delegate most directly involved in the situation because the Chopin Society, of which he was the president, operated the museum. He sent a letter on May 2 that also informed Polkowski he no longer needed to be concerned about his sister. She could continue to live on the museum site where she would receive free electricity, heat and medical care. She could also sell Chopin memorabilia to the public at Chopin's birthplace as she had done in the past. Drzewiecki explained that the problem had arisen because there had been a considerable shortfall in the accounts at the museum. While no one placed any deliberate blame on Grabowska, it was felt that she could no longer cope with the administration of a museum where the number of visitors was growing so fast. On another topic altogether, Drzewiecki indicated that the museum board had decided to erect a memorial plaque in the park at Zelazowa Wola to commemorate the work of Franciszek Krzywda Polkowski, Jozef's older brother, who had been instrumental in laying out the park site at the Chopin Museum. The concern and assistance exhibited by the members of the Polish delegation toward Mrs. Grabowska seems to reflect the mutual respect that had developed between them and the Polish expatriates during their winter sojourn in Ottawa.[328]

Around this time Halina Grabowska wrote a letter to her brother which gives an interesting glimpse into their family relationships. She was delighted to hear that Jozef might be coming to Poland. She said that there were reports about him and the collection both in the press and on television, and remarked that she was very proud of the role he had played in caring for the treasures over so many years. "May God let us see each other as soon as possible," she continued. "We are all anxiously awaiting your coming." When he reached Poland, Halina told him, they would have to settle a difficult matter with the family in Torun. It would seem that some relatives were living in a family house there, perhaps one that had belonged to their brother Franciszek. She stated that the entire place was in a shambles. What made the situation even more worrisome was the fact that the government had just passed a law permitting the confiscation of private houses that were not kept in proper repair. Halina wanted to sell the property, but finding a buyer would not be easy when one could not get rid of difficult lodgers. She felt that they would have to travel together to Torun to deal with the problem. Halina was also grateful for a parcel Polkowski had sent containing goods she could sell for cash. Because it was going to be difficult for her to travel to Warsaw to dispose of these things, she was entrusting that job to someone else. She had earmarked the extra money for the purchase of a new summer coat. In closing she sent Jozef her love and hoped that God would watch over him.[329] Rather surprisingly there was not one mention of her own employment problems in the entire letter, nor did Jozef seriously consider a trip to Poland at this time. He still had obligations to fulfill at the Provincial Museum in Quebec City.

Returning to his post at the Wawel Castle, Dr. Szablowski produced a brochure to commemorate the return of the national treasures. *The Odyssey of the National Treasures* began with a fourteen-page intro-duction describing the historic artifacts and telling the story of their sojourn in Canada. This was followed by a series of black and white illustrations of Szczerbiec, the coronation regalia and medieval manu-scripts, as well as photographs showing the opening of the trunks at the Bank of Montreal and the celebrations that accompanied their return to Poland. Hamilton Southam, the Canadian ambassador to Poland, praised the objectivity and restraint Szablowski displayed in telling the story of the national treasures. The professor, nonetheless, did conclude his presentation with a request that the remaining treasures at the Quebec Provincial Museum also be returned soon to grace the walls of the Wawel Castle.[330]

Many Polish newspapers echoed the same theme, welcoming the return of the two trunks of national treasures from the Bank of Montreal but pointing out that there still remained a vast number of historic artifacts in the province of Quebec, including the famous Wawel tapestries.

> The future chronicler of the history of our art and culture … will ponder for a long time how it happened that only in the fourteenth year after the end of the war the treasures of the Polish culture returned to the nation — and even then not all of them.…
>
> The Wawel treasures are the property of the Polish nation and no moral judgment on earth entitles the Premier of one of the Canadian provinces to decide about their destiny. Mr. Duplessis may have any view he likes as far as communism is concerned but this does not take away from him the duty to respect the property of others. Mr. Duplessis, by his attitude, not only exposes our tapestries to deterioration and harms our national culture, but also exposes to shame the good name of Canada.[331]

Another factor added urgency to the Polish requests for the return of the treasures: the millennium of the founding of the Polish state was fast approaching. Celebrations were to begin in 1960, one thousand years after Mieszko I had established his control over the Duchy of Poland. On September 10, 1959, the Polish legation wrote to the External Affairs department urging the return of the treasures in view of the preparations being made for this anniversary. A letter from representatives of the Polish academic community, with fifteen signatures and formal titles attached, also requested the return of the Polish treasures for the millennium celebrations. Even the Canadian Polish Congress echoed these sentiments.[332]

The outcry in Poland and around the world did little to soften Premier Duplessis's position. Wiktor Podoski reported that the premier would only release the Polish treasures if the London executive group requested him to do so. Duplessis's reasoning was that this group had been responsible for depositing the treasures at the Quebec museum, and therefore only it could authorize their release.[333]

* * *

The breakthrough as far as the Polish treasures were concerned came on September 7, 1959, not in Quebec City, but 1,000 kilometres to the north in the central wilderness of the province. From the time that he returned to power as premier in 1944, Duplessis had dreamed about developing the natural resources of northern Quebec and establishing an iron and steel industry in the province. The formation of the Iron Ore Company of Canada represented the first major step toward this goal. The company built a 600-kilometre railway across the tundra — from Sept-Îles on the north shore of the St. Lawrence River to Knob Lake in the interior of the province, where very large iron ore deposits had been discovered. The company built a processing plant at the head of the railway line, as well as port facilities at Sept-Îles for shipping the iron ore to steel mills in Canada and the United States.

On Wednesday, September 2, Duplessis left Quebec City to tour the premises of the Iron Ore Company. He was travelling with several political colleagues as the guests of Jules Timmins and J.H.

Thompson, the chief executives of the company. They flew first to Sept-Îles, where they toured the town in an open car, and Duplessis was very warmly received. The next day they rose early and flew north to Schefferville, the site of the great open-pit iron mines and the terminus of the railway from Sept-Îles. As soon as they arrived, most of the party departed to go fishing. Duplessis, however, stayed behind to visit the mines.

A little before lunch the premier returned to the executive guest house, which was located on a peninsula jutting out into Knob Lake. He entered the main salon and made himself comfortable chatting with one of the members of his entourage. Walking over to one of the large windows overlooking the lake, he turned to speak to his friend and suddenly collapsed, grasping his collar. The company doctor was called, and he arrived within a few minutes. He reported that Duplessis had suffered a cerebral hemorrhage, was partially paralyzed and was in very serious condition. Two specialists were flown in from Quebec City to examine Duplessis, but there was nothing that they could do. The premier possessed a strong constitution that saw him through several more days, but at midnight on Sunday the end was near. The local priest was called to administer the last rites of the church and then, very shortly thereafter, Premier Maurice Duplessis died. By this time it was early in the morning on Monday, September 7.

From Schefferville, Duplessis's body was flown to Quebec City, arriving at the airport just before the break of day. The premier's body lay in state first in the Quebec Legislative Assembly and then in the court house at Trois-Rivières. On September 10 all the members of the provincial government, the entire episcopate of the province, many representatives from other provinces, and a large delegation of federal cabinet ministers attended the funeral service at the Roman Catholic cathedral in Trois-Rivières. All concerned considered it the end of an era.[334]

* * *

For the representatives of the Warsaw government in Canada, the passing of the Duplessis era had come none too soon. With the removal of the most implacable of their adversaries, the return of the remaining Polish treasures from the Quebec Provincial Museum might be possible. Negotiations proved none too easy, however, for within the next twelve months three different leaders served as premier of Quebec. Each of them had to be approached; each had to be informed about the complex story of the Polish national treasures; each was faced with numerous other political issues that required attention. Paul Sauvé, the provincial minister of Social Welfare and Youth, was chosen as Duplessis's immediate successor. Unfortunately, he did not long outlive his predecessor and mentor. While celebrating the arrival of the new year in traditional Québécois fashion in his home riding, Sauvé suffered a heart attack. He died on January 2, 1960, at the young age of fifty-two, leaving a province in shock.[335] The next man chosen to lead the Union Nationale party and thus become premier was Antonio Barrette, a loyal party member who had served for many years as Duplessis's Labour minister. A few short months later, in June 1960, the Union Nationale was to give way in a provincial election to the Liberal party under Jean Lesage.

The attitude of the Roman Catholic Church, both in Poland and Quebec, toward the return of the Polish treasures was extremely important for all of these premiers, none of whom felt prepared to authorize their repatriation in a manner that the church would not accept. To defy the church's wishes would, after all, be political suicide in a province still staunchly Catholic. Cardinal Stefan Wyszynski, the primate of Poland, had already discussed the question of the treasures with Cardinal Paul-Emile Léger of Montreal when they met in Rome in 1957. The following year, Wyszynski sent Léger a four-page letter in which he stressed the importance of the immediate return of the treasures. He offered to take responsibility for returning them to their legal proprietor, the church, so that they might be reinstated in the Wawel Castle where they belonged. He went on to suggest that he was prepared to send a delegation with full power to reclaim the treasures and transport them back to Poland.[336]

It is difficult to understand Wyszynski's contention that the Catholic Church was the legal proprietor of the Polish treasures. The

166

Wawel tapestries, to take one major example from the collection, had been woven for a Polish king and had always been *state* property. Perhaps the cardinal was not fully conversant with all the details of the case.

Returning to the situation in January 1960, we find that Witold Malcuzynski, the Polish concert pianist, has again become involved in the negotiations concerning the fate of the Polish treasures. The ease with which he could approach the various parties involved in this repatriation process enabled him once again to make a valuable contribution toward the building of a consensus. The man who brought Malcuzynski into the negotiations for this second time was Ivan Sabourin, a Montreal lawyer who was acting as counsel for the Polish legation in Ottawa. He was also a close friend of Malcuzynski and had been involved very quietly in the pianist's earlier negotiations to repatriate the treasures from the Bank of Montreal. Malcuzynski was scheduled to give an all-Chopin concert in Quebec City on the evening of January 27. Sabourin arranged to introduce the Polish pianist to Premier Barrette at a private luncheon on the day after the concert. Sabourin's letters to the premier reveal a good deal about the interpersonal relationships between the different players in the negotiations and the way the various contacts were established.[337]

When Malcuzynski and Barrette met on January 28, the premier told Malcuzynski that he was prepared to release the Polish treasures. They went on to discuss the sending of a delegation of academics from Poland, as had been done for the earlier transfer the year before. Then, in February, Malcuzynski met in London with the executive group from the government-in-exile. This group was prepared to authorize the return of the treasures provided that it be arranged as a museum-to-museum transaction with no government involvement. They also wanted the Polish primate, Cardinal Wyszynski, to make a public statement approving the return of the national treasures to Poland. Malcuzynski was prepared to make this request of the cardinal during his next visit to Poland on March 1.[338]

The Polish church's involvement in the move to repatriate the treasures was an extremely delicate issue. Although relations between church and state were much better than they had been before 1956, they could hardly be described as cordial, and Wyszynski did not wish to do anything to aggravate the situation. The cardinal therefore told Malcuzynski that he could not make any unsolicited public statement about the Polish treasures. He asked for more time to consider the matter. When the two men met again two weeks later, Wyszynski explained that he had a solution to the problem. On Sunday, April 24, he was scheduled to attend celebrations honouring St. Wojciech, who was much revered throughout Poland. On that occasion he planned to give a speech about the Polish millennium and the longstanding connection between Poland and western Christendom. This would give him the opportunity to speak of the Wawel treasures and to express the wish that they might be returned to the Wawel as soon as possible. Malcuzynski was overwhelmed by the cardinal's decision. He proceeded to speak to several key members of the Polish government about the repatriation of the treasures. They agreed to follow the same procedure that had been used for the trunks from the Bank of Montreal and even to send the same delegates to Canada. Malcuzynski forwarded this information to the executive group in London, using a prominent private individual as a courier.[339]

Wyszynski was as good as his word. On April 24, 1960, he appeared on the balcony of his archepiscopal residence in Gniezno to speak to the thousands of pilgrims who had made the journey to honour St. Wojciech on his feast day.* During his speech the primate reported that the Polish bishops meeting in plenary conference had declared themselves in favour of the return of the national treasures to the Wawel. "All the goods that constitute the property of the nation must be returned to the nation and reinstated in their proper place," Wyszynski said. "The Wawel collections must be found at the Wawel."[340]

Talks came to a standstill when Premier Barrette called a provincial election for June 22, 1960. Barrette and the Union Nationale went down

---

*Gniezno was the first capital of Poland and the seat of the primate of the Roman Catholic Church. St. Wojciech, or St. Adalbert, was a Bohemian monk who set out on a mission to Christianize the Prussians living on the Baltic coast east of the Vistula River. He met his death at the hands of the Prussians in 997 A.D. and was canonized two years later. The oldest church in Cracow is St. Adalbert's Church, situated on the southeast corner of the town square.

to defeat, returning the Liberal party to government for the first time in sixteen years. Those seeking the transfer of the Polish national treasures would have to start from square one, educating the new government of Jean Lesage about their importance and beginning talks anew. On July 26 the Montreal *Gazette* carried Lesage's first public statement about the Polish treasures. The premier said he had no personal objection to the return of the treasures to Poland and that the matter was being turned over to the provincial Attorney General, who expected to pick up the negotiations where the previous government had left off.[341]

In August, the consul general for the Warsaw government called on Lesage in Montreal. The premier, taking his lead from Cardinal Wyszynski's letter to Cardinal Léger approximately two years before, suggested that the return of the Polish treasures be handled through the Roman Catholic Church since it owned the collection. This caused great consternation among the Warsaw Poles. Two days later the Polish chargé d'affaires in Ottawa, Mr. Sieradzki, called at the External Affairs department. He stressed that the vast majority of the Polish treasures in the Provincial Museum had never belonged to the Polish church, and that he was sure his government would never countenance the arrangement for the return of the treasures that Premier Lesage had suggested.[342] The threads of compromise that had been intricately woven together were threatening to unravel beyond repair.

Sieradzki visited New York in October to consult with the Polish minister of Foreign Affairs about the impasse. When he returned to Ottawa on October 27, he told External Affairs that the Polish government was prepared to give the government of Canada fifteen days to make the necessary arrangements for the return of the treasures. If this deadline was not met, his government would have to take independent action which would be both drastic and unpleasant from the Canadian point of view. Norman Robertson, the undersecretary of state for External Affairs, speculated that this probably meant an appeal to the International Court of Justice.[343]

External Affairs moved quickly. On November 4 a telegram to its Warsaw office requested a clarification of the opinion expressed by Cardinal Wyszynski concerning the ownership of the Polish treasures and how they could best be returned.[344] At this point the Canadian representative in Warsaw, Hamilton Southam, became a key player in the international negotiations. A scion of the newspaper publishing family, Southam had been appointed to Warsaw only eighteen months before. He now approached Wyszynski through a senior member of the Znak Catholic parliamentary party. Within two days Southam had received Wyszynski's reply in the form of a letter to Cardinal Léger. Having been informed verbally of the contents of this letter, Southam immediately sent a telegram to External Affairs explaining the cardinal's current views: Wyszynski had agreed that the national treasures be returned to Poland through representatives of the Wawel Museum without any involvement by the Polish church. The cardinal did express the view, however, that someone from the Roman Catholic Church in Canada should be present when the transfer took place. Having received this communication from Southam, Norman Robertson at External Affairs recommended that the department proceed to contact the interested parties on the basis of this information from Warsaw, although the final steps toward a transfer of the treasures would have to await the arrival of Cardinal Wyszynski's letter.[345] By the end of the month, everything was in place; on November 29 Southam was able to inform the Polish ministry of Foreign Affairs that representatives of the Wawel could proceed to Quebec to secure the release of the Polish national treasures.[346]

* * *

This news reached Adam Zurowski approximately two weeks later. Antoine Roy, the director of the Provincial Museum, telephoned to say that a delegation from Warsaw was due to arrive in Quebec on December 27. Roy was somewhat distraught, as he did not have any idea what items the Polish collection contained, and he said he could not proceed without Zurowski's participation.[347] When December 23 arrived and he had still received no invitation to the impending transaction, Zurowski approached Lester Pearson, who was astonished at this oversight on the part of the provincial administration. Pearson immediately telephoned Premier Lesage, who explained that he had instructed Roy to forward the invitation to Zurowski. Lesage now personally put things right by inviting both Zurowski and Polkowski to the meetings in Quebec City.[348]

Polkowski described what happened at the Quebec gathering in considerable detail, beginning in this way:

> I left at once, and the same day, at eleven o'clock in the evening I arrived in Quebec to stay in the same hotel as usual. The following day, at nine in the morning, I was informed that a police car was waiting for me, which was to take me to the headquarters of the Provincial Police. It was obvious that the police had been tracking my movements. I was taken to headquarters, where the commander of the investigating police … without exchanging greetings with me, asked if I had the inventory book of the collection. I answered that I had such a book in Ottawa, but on me I only had a list of what was to be found in Quebec. He ordered me to show it. When I did this, he seized it from my hand and said that after a copy had been made it would be given back.
>
> That night Mr. Adam Zurowski arrived from Ottawa, and the receiving group flew in from Warsaw. This group was composed of: the Director of the Wawel, Prof. Jerzy Szablowski; Prof. Bohdan Marconi; and the secretary of the Wawel directorate, Mrs. Anna Godzicka; as well as four Wawel workmen, who had worked in the Wawel since pre-war times. [Actually, these workmen had helped man the barge that had carried the Wawel artifacts down the Vistula River on the first leg of their journey in 1939.]
>
> When I was driven to the Museum [on the next day], waiting for us was our old friend, the head of the investigative police in Quebec and the former "body guard" of the deceased Premier Duplessis, Mr. Duchesnay. He was called there to open the doors, since only he knew the secret for the opening of the

armoured doors to the vault where the collection was kept. After the vault was opened, I was not permitted to enter, being told that only policemen had the right of entry. When Director Szablowski and Director Roy arrived, I protested at this decree, because only I knew where each object lay and in what order, and could prevent possible damage. After lengthy negotiations with the police I was eventually permitted to enter the vault, on the condition, however, that I would not touch anything and would only direct the work of the policemen.

We were treated as thieves and bandits. During all this work I was forbidden to take anything out of the chests, but only permitted to open them. Messrs. Roy and Szablowski looked on at this behaviour of the policemen with disgust, but they adhered to the orders received from that brutal director of provincial police, who had specially arrived from Montreal.

The work of returning the collection took place very quickly. I noted each item in my inventory lists, Mr. Szablowski did the same in his own, while the workmen shut the chests once more. Professor Marconi was responsible for ensuring that the objects were properly placed in the chests.... Late in the afternoon of the thirty-first of December the handing over of the collection was finished. After the signing of my inventory lists by Director Szablowski with the note that he had received everything according to these lists and in good order, we went to a joint supper. Unfortunately this meal was without wine, because the then idiotic Quebec regulations forbade the selling of alcoholic beverages on that day [New Year's Eve].[349]

The Polish delegation had arrived on Wednesday, the examination of the artifacts took place on Thursday and Friday, and the signing of the documents officially transferring the Polish treasures occurred on

Saturday, December 31. Present at the official signing, which took place in the office of the director of the Provincial Museum, were: representing Poland, Dr. Jerzy Szablowski, director of the Wawel Museum, and Dr. Bogdan Marconi, chief conservator of historical artifacts; from the province of Quebec, Antoine Roy, provincial archivist and director of the Provincial Museum; Charles Cantin, deputy Attorney General of Quebec; Lieutenant Colonel Lambert, director of the Quebec Provincial Police; Père Rondeau, representing Archbishop Maurice Roy of the Quebec diocese; and, representing the executive group of London Poles, Adam Zurowski, trustee for the treasures, and Jozef Polkowski, curator of the treasures.

The signing process was completed by a guarantee from the Polish government that neither the province of Quebec nor the Provincial Museum would be held responsible for any claims of damage to the treasures.[350] And so the Poles got back their national treasures before the end of 1960 — their millennium year of celebration — but only by a hair's breadth!

CHAPTER TWENTY-THREE
The Homecoming

The Polish treasures would have left Quebec City on New Year's Day except that a nasty winter storm blew up, delaying their departure for twenty-four hours. Consequently, it was on Monday evening, January 2, that police blocked the approaches to the Provincial Museum on the Plains of Abraham so that the treasures could be placed aboard two large vans for the trip from Quebec City to Boston. Once the trunks were in place and the vans had been sealed, the small convoy got under way at 10:30 p.m., with the RCMP assuming the task of guarding the shipment as far as the U.S. border. The icy roads were still partially covered with snow, forcing the vehicles to move at a snail's pace, seldom exceeding 60 kilometres per hour. At the request of the truck drivers they stopped twice during the night for coffee breaks, finally reaching the border at Rock Island, in the Eastern Townships of Quebec, at 5:15 a.m. After the RCMP checked the seals on the vans, they drove on a few hundred more yards to cross the border at Derby Line, Vermont. There, American police took over the duty of escorting the Polish treasures on their way to Boston[351] (see Map VIII).

The visit of the Polish delegation to Quebec City and the release of the Polish treasures had taken place without any publicity. Secrecy continued to be well maintained until the evening of the departure from Quebec, when Adam Zurowski issued a statement to the press that left the rest of the participants in the negotiations scrambling to catch up.[352] Newspapermen were immediately on the trail of a story, and by the time the convoy had reached the border on Tuesday morning, reporters were on hand seeking interviews. The headline in the Montreal *Star* on January 3 read "Twenty Year Dispute Settled; Treasures Cross Border at Rock Island." The following day, the Ottawa *Journal* carried a report from the Canadian Press that featured an interview with Walter Duchesnay, the guardian of the Polish treasures at the Provincial Museum. Duchesnay had kept his story to himself for twelve years, but this is what the CP reporter finally revealed about his participation:

> Mr. Duchesnay, a blue-eyed, white-haired special officer with the attorney-general's department, was the man who carried out Mr. Duplessis's orders Feb. 28, 1948 [actually February 25], although he had no inkling he was arranging the transport of a controversial treasure.
>
> "Mr. Duplessis called me one day and told me to take a letter to the superior of the Hôtel-Dieu Hospital. The mother superior read the letter and asked who Duchesnay was. 'That's me,' I replied.
>
> "The mother rang a bell and a little sister came and escorted me through dark corridors and staircases until we were finally in a stone cellar. She showed me 24 trunks and said: 'Here it is.'
>
> "I went back to Mr. Duplessis and he told me: 'Get them out of there before 4:00 p.m. I don't care how you do it, get them out. Bring them to the museum. Take all necessary precautions. This is highly secret and there is a fortune in those trunks.' ...
>
> No other man knew the combination of the provincial museum vault where the historical relics were kept.... Even after the death of Mr. Duplessis in September 1959 and the change of government last June, Mr. Duchesnay held the combination of the secret lock, built according to his specifications after the treasures were placed in the custody of the provincial government in 1948.
>
> Tuesday night, after the treasures had been packed into two trucks, Mr. Duchesnay locked the heavy steel

door into place and bid Polish government representatives goodbye. Mr. Duchesnay's special assignment
was completed.[353]

The shipment of Polish treasures arrived in Boston late in the
day on January 3. On the following day the collection was loaded
aboard the Polish freighter *Krynica*, bound for the Baltic port of
Gdynia, and it sailed by midafternoon.[354] Several of the key people
aboard ship spoke by radio to the Polish Press Agency (PAP) a few
nights later. First, Professor Jerzy Szablowski told his audience that all
was going well. He explained that the national treasures had been
stored in the crew's dining room for safekeeping. All the crates and
trunks had been carefully filled with insulation to protect any art
objects against the rolling of the ship. These containers were also
tightly wrapped in heavy plastic to prevent water from seeping inside.
The captain of the *Krynica* commented that the ship was rolling
strongly, but he described the weather they were encountering as an
ordinary storm. He assured his Polish listeners that his crew would
have no trouble bringing the national treasures safely back home. In
a second radio interview on January 10, Szablowski reported that
they were following the most direct route across the Atlantic and
planned to enter the Baltic Sea through the Danish Straits instead of
the Kiel Canal. The professor reported that the weather was clear,
but with a strong wind still blowing that made for rough seas. He said
that the captain had already announced that *Krynica* would enter
port decked out in full regalia.[355]

The ship reached Gdynia's harbour on the afternoon of Sunday,
January 15, but did not berth for unloading until the following day.
Peter Scott, one of the foreign-service officers at the Canadian embassy
in Warsaw, was sent to attend the celebration marking the return of the
Polish treasures. He described the morning's events in the following
terms in his report to the Canadian ambassador:

> My wife and I arrived at the waterfront at 8:10 a.m.,
> some twenty minutes before the arrival of the ship itself.
> No public announcement had been made of the exact

time and place of the ship's arrival. If there had been such an announcement, it was later explained to us, the crowds at the dockside would have been uncontrollable. As it was there must have been somewhere between 1,000 and 1,500 people crowded behind the wooden fences of the docks, or up on the parapets and roof of the terminal building. Some of these were school children who had been specially supplied with flowers, Polish flags, and banners welcoming the treasures return. The terminal itself, usually a rather depressing building, was decked out with large bright red banners. One of these told us "The Priceless Historic Treasures are Returning to their Rightful Owner — the Polish Nation." Another, in the same vein: "Only the Fatherland is the proper Place for National Souvenirs." Special policemen were directing the traffic outside.

Even the cobbles and rails of the dockside, seen from the milling crowd on the parapets, had the air of a serious and festive occasion. At one end stood a team of firemen with brightly polished helmets and a gleaming wagon of fire extinguishers. Beside them were the special volunteer team of longshoremen, in freshly washed denims and new leather gloves. (They donated their pay on this special occasion, as you know, towards a "millennium school.") Upwards of thirty or forty cameramen — press, film and television — were running to and fro, climbing the cranes, leaping onto railway wagons, or holding their movie cameras over the heads of the crowd. But the chief place was taken by four Pullman saloon coaches whose honour it was to be to convey the treasures to Warsaw. In front of these was a twenty piece band; and, in front of the band, a small group of shivering officials gathered around a microphone....

When I mentioned that my wife and I were from the Canadian Embassy, we were quickly ushered out onto the dockside with a smile. There were no loudspeakers, and thus I am a little uncertain as to the order of ceremonies at the outset. Almost immediately the *Krynica* came into view and was quickly berthed; whereupon we all stood at attention to the jubilant strains of the Polish national anthem. Many other people then pressed with us to the side of the ship: a delegation of Wawel workers (headed by Mr. Majewski, the chief Wawel architect), the families of the officers and crew, and so on. One group, pointed out to me later, consisted of the bus drivers and transport workers in whose care the treasures had been shipped out of Poland in 1939. They reportedly watched the treasures' return with tears in their eyes....

[Later] the trunks of the treasures were being moved out of the Officers' Mess [sic], their home for the last ten days, onto the rear deck, whence they were carefully lifted to shore by crane, in a specially constructed padded felt frame. Blankets covered the trunks as they were moved, and large quantities of corrugated paperboard were used to bed the trunks down in the train.... Professors Szablowski and Marconi followed every movement of the longshoremen with passionate attention; while the firemen were kept busy for the next hour or so preventing the reporters from smoking....

[Once] the treasures were safely aboard their train ... we decided it was time for us to slip quietly away, which we did just at precisely the same time as the treasures themselves; we for a short visit to Szczecin, the treasures for Warsaw.[356]

The train carrying the national treasures arrived in Warsaw at 9:30 in the evening of January 16. Here the time of arrival had been announced in the press and there were crowds at the Central Station awaiting the train. It was a cold, wintry night with a strong wind, so people were stamping their feet and turning up their collars as they waited. By 9:30 the crowd on the platform was so dense that one could hardly move. People with banners, photographers, and delegations bearing flowers jostled with passengers hoping to catch the express train for points beyond Warsaw. Eventually, the four Pullman coaches with their special cargo were detached from the train, which continued on its way. The crowd moved aside for the railway trolleys to approach. Then workers spread rugs on the trolleys and placed thick sheets of paper on the rugs. Around 11:00 p.m., after the public had been warned again to move back and to put out their cigarettes, the first trunk emerged — a dark green one, reinforced with metal and sealed. Numerous trunks, a large chest, and sixteen cloth rolls were unloaded and taken to large furniture vans lined with padded mattresses that were waiting outside the railway station. People were still crowding the area around the station and along Aleja Jerozolimskie to watch the treasures depart. It was almost midnight before the last cloth roll, packed in thick white linen and also sealed, was transferred to a van. Motors in the vans and in the automobile escorts were started and the motorcade moved off — furniture vans in the middle, escorts in front, at the sides and in the rear — all moving along Aleja Jerozoslimskie to the National Museum.[357]

When Professors Szablowski and Marconi opened the trunks and containers at the National Museum the next day, they commented on the condition of the Polish treasures. In an interview with a reporter from the Polish Press Agency they stated that the Provincial Museum in Quebec City had treated the priceless objects with great consideration. For storage purposes the tapestries had indeed been lain on top of one another, which was not good conservation practice, but this was the result of lack of space and in no way reflected ill will on the part of the management or employees at the museum. On the contrary, the Quebec Provincial Museum had done everything in its power to protect the treasures from damage despite their long years in storage. The professors concluded that the collection was in reasonably good condition and that, after appropriate conservation work, the treasures would once again adorn the Wawel as magnificently as they had in years gone by.[358]

Searching for colourful background material concerning the Polish treasures, a reporter from the *Trybuna Ludu* discovered

Franciszek Misia, the owner of the coal barge that had removed the treasures from the Wawel Castle in 1939. This was his report:

> In the raftsman village of Laczany near Cracow lives a certain Franciszek Misia who, on September 3, 1939, transported the Wawel treasures out of the endangered town on his own Vistula galley.
>
> "I remember everything as if it had just happened," says Misia. "We loaded 21 boxes, 7 rolls with arrases and one big roll with banners on the galley. The shipment was accompanied by the director of the collections at the Wawel Castle, Professor Swierz Zaleski, and by many other people from the Castle and even from the town. In addition to the relics there were on the galley more than 80 people including some children.
>
> We set sail at night and went down the river. When we arrived near Sandomierz, German bombers bombed the town and the bridges. They also took our galley as a target.... However the true danger started near Solec. Here the Vistula River formed the front-line. On one side of the Vistula were the Germans and on the other side were our soldiers defending themselves. So we sailed under artillery fire from Solec to Kasimierz.[359]

Franciszek Misia concluded the interview by saying that he would like to see the relics back at the Wawel Castle. Both Misia and Leopold Pisz, the postmaster at Kasimierz who had secured land transport for the treasures in 1939, had received the Golden Cross of Merit from the Polish government for their part in the rescue operation.[360] For Pisz, this honour came posthumously, since he had died during the war at the hands of the Nazi occupation forces. Dr. Szablowski had sent a letter from the Wawel Castle to Pisz's wife praising her husband's valour in those dark days of 1939. He also reported that Franciszek Misia had twice visited the Wawel to pay his respects to the staff there.[361]

* * *

Local politics can exercise a powerful influence on national affairs, even in such a highly centralized political system as that of the Polish People's Republic. Before the treasures had even arrived at Gdynia, the director of the National Museum in Warsaw touched off a political tug-of-war between Cracow and Warsaw concerning the ownership of the national treasures. Dr. Lorenz claimed that some of the celebrated Flemish tapestries should remain in Warsaw, either at the National Museum or at Warsaw's Royal Palace, which was scheduled to be rebuilt. He argued that the tapestries had spent very few years of their long history at the Wawel Castle in Cracow. At times they had accompanied the Polish kings as they travelled from castle to castle around Poland. For long periods they had been outside the country altogether — in Russia during the nineteenth century and in Canada more recently. Lorenz did not see any reason why some of the returning tapestries should not grace the walls of buildings in the capital of Poland. Szablowski, a director of the Wawel Castle, on the other hand, expected the Flemish tapestries to be returned there. The arrases had been designed originally to fit the walls of the Wawel. Later, when they were repatriated from Russia, they were once again placed in the royal castle to adorn the walls for which they had been originally designed. It was from the Wawel Castle that they had been removed in 1939, starting off on that series of adventures that took them halfway around the world. As far as Szablowski was concerned, the arrases should be returned to their ancestral home.

This dispute between the two academics was well depicted in a contemporary cartoon that showed Professors Lorenz and Szablowski tugging away at opposite ends of a tapestry with no regard for the fabric they were tearing apart. Dr. Lorenz seems to have overstepped the mark when he submitted a memorandum to the politburo advocating his point of view. Perhaps he overlooked the fact that Prime Minister Cyrankiewicz, a leading member of the politburo, was a native of Cracow and a stout defender of his hometown's interests. At any rate his memorandum was rejected. The tapestries returned to Cracow.[362]

Lorenz did win approval for an exhibition of the treasures at the National Museum before they travelled on to Cracow. The exhibition opened on January 25 with Mr. Galinski, the minister of Culture, as host. Ambassador Southam, representing the Canadian government, thought that it was not nearly as brilliant an affair as he had been led to expect. Perhaps the dispute over the ownership of the treasures cast a shadow over the proceedings, or perhaps it was because the principal celebration in connection with the return of the treasures was to take place at the Wawel in mid-March. In any case, Southam described the reception which he attended that evening in the following terms:

> The speeches of Professor Lorenz and Mr. Galinski were short and to the point. Both made only passing references to Canada. Then a ribbon was cut and we surged into the rooms ... where some of the tapestries were hung. They are a glorious sight, far more beautiful than I had imagined they could be, shimmering as they do with gold thread. As far as my unpractised eye could determine, there was no sign of damage whatever, and in fact the experts have stated publicly here that there was none attributable to their stay in Canada, although apparently rain water got at parts of two or three of them at an early stage in their journey thither. I was delighted to see all the professors who had played a role in the treasures' story, Morelowski, Marconi and Szablowski, the last named keeping well clear of Professor Lorenz. It was, as you can imagine, a happy occasion, and never have I heard so many kind things said about my country as during the hour or so we spent there.
>
> In the evening Professor Morelowski gave a lecture on the tapestries at the Palace of Culture. I was not able to go but my wife represented the Canadian Embassy, and to her surprise heard our friend launch into a flattering speech about her and Canada before an audience of several hundred people, who applauded vigorously as

a little girl emerged from somewhere and presented her with flowers. The lecture was accompanied by slides and took much longer than planned because Professor Morelowski translated everything he had to say into French for my wife's sole benefit. She found it all very touching and more than a little embarrassing.[363]

By the time this report was being forwarded to Canada, the exhibition had been open for three weeks. The National Museum staff told Southam that more than 260,000 people had seen the treasures thus far and the exhibition still had more than a week to run. On one Sunday afternoon an all-time record of 35,300 visitors pressed through the exhibition halls at the museum.[364] The Polish people were once again welcoming back their national treasures with enthusiasm.

Opening night for the exhibition at the Wawel Castle had been billed as the major celebration marking the return of the treasures to Poland; however, it too turned out to be remarkably low key. Neither President Gomulka nor Prime Minister Cyrankiewicz was in attendance, nor were Cardinal Wyszinski or the Archbishop of Cracow present at the ceremony. Searching for some explanation for the change in plans, the Canadian ambassador suggested three possibilities. The decision could have been triggered by the rivalry between Cracow and Warsaw; it could have been a reaction against the strong upsurge of Polish national feeling aroused by the return of the treasures; or it could have been a reflection of the recent stiffening of the Soviet bloc's attitude toward the NATO countries. At any rate, according to Hamilton Southam, the evening proceeded as follows:

We arrived at the Wawel at the time indicated on the invitations, 6:00 p.m., only to find that the speeches were nearly over. Mr. Galinski's was extremely short.... He then took my hand briefly without saying anything as he walked briskly towards the doorway which opened onto the rooms where the tapestries had been hung. Once past that starting point ... he began a break-neck tour of the exhibition with which I was quite unable to keep up. In less than an hour Mr. Galinski disappeared as suddenly as though he had fallen into one of the oubliettes of the castle, and the reception was over....

It was quite obvious that Professor Szablowski and his Wawel staff were taken aback by what looked very much like the deliberate sabotage of their great evening by the Minister of Culture. It was he who played the host — or rather didn't — and the invitation list had been in his hands. The young lady who showed us round told us that Professor Szablowski had expected far more guests to come from Warsaw — distinguished political figures and all the ambassadors.[365]

Just before the ambassador left the castle, Professor Szablowski presented him with a book entitled *Studies in the History of the Wawel* as an expression of his profound gratitude, sympathy and respect. And so ended that evening's festivities.[366] Southam summed up the many months of diplomatic manoeuvring by saying that it was extremely unlikely that he would ever again in his career as a diplomat have to deal with a question as passionately interesting as that of the Polish treasures.[367]

* * *

While these festivities were taking place in Poland, the Warsaw Symphony Orchestra was touring North America. On February 6, at a concert in Ottawa, the orchestra played Chopin's Second Piano Concerto as an addition to the repertoire it had presented elsewhere. The conductor explained that the concerto was being played to express the orchestra's thanks for the repatriation of the many historic Polish national treasures, including the original handwritten manuscript of this particular piece.[368] His tribute is a fitting denouement to the three celebrations honouring the return of the Polish treasures — the end of a strange odyssey.

CHAPTER TWENTY-FOUR
Postlude

Jozef Polkowski still had in hand an invitation from his friends, Dr. Szablowski and Dr. Morelowski, to visit them in Poland. The Polish government, moreover, offered him first-class passage for the voyage across the Atlantic and a pass for the Polish national railways during his stay. There was criticism, however, from some members of the Polish-Canadian community who thought Polkowski was about to accept favours from the communist government,[369] and Polkowski ultimately paid for his own transatlantic passage and rail travel. Adam Zurowski commented that Polkowski was using all his savings to pay for the trip to Poland, which was bound to make life difficult for him upon his return to Canada.[370]

On April 22, 1961, Polkowski sailed for Poland on the MS *Batory*, the same Polish liner that had brought him to Canada twenty-one years before.[371] Upon his arrival he was the guest of Dr. Jerzy Szablowski at the Wawel Castle, where he could see the Polish national treasures displayed in all their splendour — tapestries on the walls for which they had been designed, Szczerbiec in a glass case in the Treasury Room where it could be seen to advantage from every angle. Polkowski must have rejoiced that the treasures he had safeguarded for so long were once again back where they belonged. The elderly curator commented on the report of the conservation commission that had been established to investigate the state of the collection upon its return to Poland. The commission had concluded that the national treasures must have been properly cared for in Canada because they had indeed arrived home in excellent condition. Polkowski considered this endorsement a fitting reward for the years of trouble and criticism he had endured while attending to the collection in Canada. In addition, he received letters from Polish art historians and conservators as well as from student organizations thanking him for saving the national treasures. The comments of the students were, for Polkowski, the most cherished of all the communications he received.[372]

Jozef Polkowski still felt strong ties to the country of his birth, but he no longer wanted to live there under the conditions he had witnessed on his trip. He was not prepared to put up with the censorship, the lack of freedom and the scarcity of international news that he experienced in his homeland. When he had first arrived in Canada, the country had seemed strange to him; he had found it necessary to adjust to a different lifestyle, a different landscape and a different climate. Because he could not work at his profession, Polkowski had not benefited materially from his years in Canada. Nevertheless, he chose to return to his adopted country, although he advised that no one should immigrate to Canada without a profession or a skilled trade to support him.[373]

When Polkowski returned to Ottawa, he resumed work at the European Delicatessen, putting in a six-day week for $30 in pay. He continued to work there until his seventy-ninth birthday, six years later. By this time he was receiving his old-age pension, which he managed to live on with a supplement from the Department of Veterans Affairs. For many years he had continued to live in the duplex on First Avenue in Ottawa's Glebe neighbourhood that he shared with his good friends, the Newlands family. Then, probably sometime in 1958, he moved into rented rooms, where he stayed for some years until he got an apartment in a senior citizens' home at 395 Somerset Street West.[374]

Jozef Aleksander Polkowski died on October 11, 1981, at the age of ninety-three. He was buried in Notre Dame Cemetery and, in lieu of flowers, friends were asked to donate to the Polish National Fund or to the Sikorski Museum in London, England.[375]

Stanisláw Swierz Zaleski, Polkowski's colleague on the voyage to Canada, had returned to Poland in September 1948. He received no mark of recognition upon his return, nor was there any work for him at the Wawel Castle, where he had been employed before the war. Zaleski had been a party to the hiding away of the treasures by the London

186

Poles in 1945; thereafter he had defected to the Warsaw side and told Dr. Fiderkiewicz, the Polish chargé d'affaires, where the treasures had been hidden. When the Polish authorities searched the premises Zaleski had identified, however, the treasures were no longer there. Consequently, Zaleski did not rate very highly with the communist regime in Poland. He was, nonetheless, respected by his professional colleagues at the Wawel Castle, some of whom would have known him prior to 1939. With their assistance he secured a position as professor at the Academy of Fine Arts in Cracow.[376] Swierz Zaleski died at his country home in Zakopane on September 22, 1951, three years after his return to Poland. He was sixty-five years old.[377]

* * *

In February 2001 the Musée du Quebec* mounted an exhibition, *The Return of the Polish Treasures*, to commemorate the fortieth anniversary of the departure of the Polish treasures. The bulletin of the Musée du Quebec described the exhibition.

The Return of the Polish Treasures: Royal Splendour

It is indeed a question of a return! Forty years after their departure from Quebec, the exhibition brings back the Polish treasures to the Museum and lifts the veil on this fascinating story. You will be able to follow the resurrection of this adventure story in a well illustrated publication. In Rooms 5 and 6 of the Museum you will discover a significant part of these collections which transport us to the royal Wawel Castle in Cracow and immerse us in the ambience of the sixteenth, seventeenth and eighteenth centuries. Joined with Lithuania, Poland was then an important realm at the crossroads of East and West. Eight of the

*The Musée du Quebec was known as the Quebec Provincial Museum in the 1940s.

tapestries which adorned the castle during the holding of great events are now suspended from the mouldings of the Museum, offering to the visitor a spectacle of royal splendour. Broadswords and armour, chests, cabinets, currency and, of course, paintings and portraits complete this unique collection which reveals to us brilliantly the importance of these coveted treasures.

The exhibition is presented with the collaboration of the royal Wawel Castle.[378]

Anyone fortunate enough to have attended the exhibition would have had to agree that it did indeed provide a rewarding glimpse of the marvellous Polish national treasures that Canada sheltered in its midst for twenty-one controversial years.

ACKNOWLEDGEMENTS

First of all, I wish to thank my students and colleagues at Nicholas Copernicus High School in Warsaw for a very positive two-year teaching experience in Poland. In 1994 my wife and I agreed to teach English conversation at Nicolas Copernicus, where I was also asked to teach my own subject, history, to two senior International Baccalaureate classes. Because teaching these students was a real pleasure, we returned to the school two more times in the 1990s. It was this connection with Poland that eventually led to the writing of this Polish-Canadian story.

The research for the book began in Quebec City. There I would like to acknowledge the kind assistance of Sister Marie-Paule Cauchon, the archivist of the Augustine Sisters at the Hôtel-Dieu. She not only opened their files on the Polish treasures for my use, but also gave me a tour of that part of the convent where the treasures had been hidden in the mid-1940s. The staff at the Archives nationales du Quebec was also very helpful, as were Jocelyn St. Pierre and his colleagues at the Archives of the Assemblée Nationale.

The staff at the National Archives of Canada, where I did the bulk of my research work, were always ready to make available their many documents on the Polish Art Treasures. Their service was excellent. The Ottawa *Citizen* and Ottawa *Journal*, as well as other periodicals such as *Maclean's*, were available on microfilm at the National Library of Canada. The help of the staff there was also greatly appreciated. The Embassy of the Republic of Poland in Ottawa has given its encouragement and support throughout the project. I would like to thank particularly Tomasz Moszczynski, the cultural attaché at the embassy, for his help in tracking down addresses of Polish photographers and publishers for me and for answering many other questions.

At the Sikorski Institute in London, and in Poland, I needed the help of a translator to deal with Polish documents. Michael Kulczykowski undertook this service for me at the Sikorski Institute, where the staff once again proved most helpful. Artur Kuzma translated for me in Warsaw. There we consulted the Archives of the Ministry of Foreign Affairs with the assistance of Bogusláw Winid and Pawel Bogdziewicz; the National Library with the help of Mariola Nalecz and Meria Wrede; and the Chopin Institute, where Hanna Wrobleska-Straus was our mentor and guide. Jan Krzewinski did further research in Poland for me after my return to Canada and Jacek Stolcman helped with the translation of Jozef Polkowski's Long Memoir. Artur, Jan and Jacek were all students from Nicholas Copernicus High School. My heartfelt thanks goes to them and to Michael Kulczykowski. I could not have done the Polish research work without them.

The excellent map work was done by Suzanne Dodge and Associates of Prescott, Ontario. Thank you, Suzanne. I would also like to thank all the staff at Dundurn Press, whose cooperation throughout the publication process was much appreciated.

Finally, I would like to acknowledge the debt that I owe to my parents. Their love of reading and respect for education, their interest in world affairs and their openness to people of many different backgrounds became unconsciously a part of my psyche. Without these interests this book would never have been written.

BIBLIOGRAPHY

CANADIAN SOURCES

PRIMARY SOURCES:

ARCHIVES DE L'ASSEMBLÉ NATIONALE DU QUÉBEC:
Les extraits des journaux dont on est en train de reconstruire les débats de l'assemblé.

Articles sur les trésors polonais — 3, 4, 5, 11 mars 1948;

Debats en Chambre (trésors polonais) — 4, 22, 23 mars 1948.

ARCHIVES NATIONALES DU QUÉBEC:
File # ANQ-Q, E53, V.1919-00-006/57;

File # P688, S3, SS9/ #367 Trésors polonais, 1939–61;

Conseil executif 03Q–E5 (#2 C 030 04-06-004B-01/2.1 trésors polonais; ANQ-Q-E53 (versement 1919-00-006-57).

ARCHIVES DES SOEURS AUGUSTINES DE LA MISÉRICORDE DE JÉSUS, HÔTEL-DIEU DU QUÉBEC:
Les trésors polonais, Tiroir 11 — C960;

Aussi beaucoup de dossiers des extraits des journaux.

NATIONAL ARCHIVES OF CANADA:
RG 25 — External Affairs, File #837-40 — Polish treasures:

Vol. 2803 ...1 (24 June 1940 — 31 July 1947)

Vol. 3555 ...2, 3, 4 (28 July 1947 — 31 Aug. 1949)

Vol. 6182 ...5.1, 5.2 (1Sept. 1949 — 26 Apr. 1951)

Vol. 6341 …6, 7 (15 May 1951 — 22 June 1955)
Vol. 6769 …8, 9, 10 (12 May 1955 — 30 Apr. 1958)
Vol. 6770 …10, 11-13.1 (6 May 1958 — 15 Oct. 1959)
Vol. 6771 …13.2 (15 Oct. 1959 — 29 Feb. 1960)
Vol. 5022 …14, 15, 16 (2 Mar. 1960 — 6 June 1963)
RG 25 — External Affairs, File #837-B-40 — Polish treasures / legal aspects:
Vol. 2803 …1 (11 July 1940 — 27 Dec. 1956)
Vol. 6771 …2, 3, 3A (29 Sept. 1947 — 24 May 1962)
RG 25 — External Affairs, File #9396-40
Vol. 3912 …1 (3 July 1945 — 5 Feb. 1947)
RG 2 — Privy Council Office:
Vol. 5775 (8 Mar. 1956 — 19 Dec. 1956)
Vol. 1898 (4 January 1958 — 15 July 1958)
MG 28 — Manuscript Division:
Vol. 79-1: Polkowski's Long Memoir (62 pp.)
Polkowski's Short Memoir (17 pp.)
RG 18 — Royal Can. Mounted Police, File # 1946-HQ-1046-A-1:
Vol. 6094 …1, 2, 3 (21 May 1946 — 9 January 1961)
NAC Reference Section — Photographs from Adam Zurowski Collection, Accession # 1993-359.

NATIONAL GALLERY OF CANADA / LIBRARY AND ARCHIVES:
Catalogue for Exhibition of Polish Art / NGC, Ottawa, 1942 — File # 1942 Polish Art (NGC exhibitions / documentation file).

SECONDARY SOURCES:

BOOKS:

Balawyder, Aloysius. *The Odyssey of the Polish Treasures*. Antigonish, N.S.: St. Francis Xavier Press, 1978.

Black, Conrad. *Duplessis*. Toronto: McClelland & Stewart, 1977.

Davies, Nicholas. *God's Playground: A History of Poland*. Toronto: Clarendon Press, 1981.

Gielzynski, Wojciech, and Irena & Jerzy Kostrowicki, *Poland*, trans. Peter Martin. Warsaw: Arkady Publishing House, 1994.

Ostrowski, Ian, and Jon Porter: *Le retour des trésors polonais*, Catalogue for the exhibitionof the same name at the Musée du Québed, 2001.

Roberts, Leslie. *The Chief: A Political Biography of Maurice Duplessis*. Toronto: Clarke, Irwin, 1963.

Sadie, Stanley, ed. *New Grove Dictionary of Music and Musicians*. See esp. entry on "Malcuzynski." London: Macmillan, 1980.

Salter, Mark, and Gordon McLachlan. *Poland: The Rough Guide*, 2nd ed. London: Rough Guides, 1993.

Syrop, Konrad. *Poland: Between the Hammer and the Anvil*. London: Hale, 1968.

Zamoyski, Adam: *The Polish Way: A Thousand-Year History of the Poles and Their Culture*. London: John Murray, 1987.

BROCHURES:

Lorenz, Stanisláw. *Canada Refuses to Return Polish Cultural Treasures*. Warsaw: National Museum, 1949 (at NAC, RG25, 837-40, 6770 ...10FP1.2).

Szablowski, Jerzy. *Odyseja Skarbow Narodowych (The Odyssey of the National Treasures)*. Cracow: Wawel Museum, 1960 (at NAC, RG25, 837-40, 5022 ...14).

ARTICLES:

Egan, Kelly. "The Amazing Saga of Poland's Treasures." *Ottawa Citizen*, August 29, 1999.

Guzowska, M. "King Sigismund Augustus' Treasures." *Kaleidoscope* [LOT's in-flight magazine], April 30, 1986.

Hollier, Robert. "En Pologne on les appelle les trésors du Canada." *Le Magazine Maclean*, September 1962.

Karsh, Yousuf. "Quebec." *Maclean's*, December 1, 1953.

———. "The Polish Art Treasures." *Life*, December 14, 1953.

———. "The Polish Art Treasures: A Gift from Yousuf Karsh." *Maclean's*. December 15, 1953.

Mazurkowa, J. "Engineer Jozef Krzyda Polkowski, the Faithful Custodian of the Wawel Treasures." *Polish Historical Society in Great Britain's Historical Papers* Vol. 21 (1994–1995): 289–302.

Mitric, T.D. "Guarding the Gold." *The Beaver*, October–November 2000.

Nalecz, M. "Chopin's Manuscripts in the Collection of the National Library in Warsaw." *Chopin in the World* (1999): 18–21.

Petrus, Jerzy T. "L'Odyssée des trésors polonais," in *Le retour des trésors polonais*. Quebec: Musée du Québec, 2001.

Porter, John. "De Cracovie à Québec," in *Le retour des trésors polonais*. Quebec: Musée du Québec, 2001.

Porter, Mackenzie. "Who's Going to Get the Polish Art Treasures?" *Maclean's*, July 15, 1953.

NEWSPAPERS: (ON MICROFILM AT THE NATIONAL LIBRARY OF CANADA)

Ottawa Citizen, November 7–30, 1946; February 25–March 31, 1948.
Ottawa Journal, for the same dates as above.

There are also many newspaper articles in the RG25 files at the National Archives of Canada. These were clipped from Canadian papers by employees of the Department of External Affairs or sent to the department from the Canadian legation in Poland, usually accompanied by an English translation.

POLISH SOURCES

PRIMARY SOURCES:

ARCHIVES OF THE CHOPIN INSTITUTE, WARSAW:

Zaleska, Josefa: *Franciszek Krzyda Polkowski, 1881-1949* (an unpublished memoir).

ARCHIVES OF THE MINISTRY OF FOREIGN AFFAIRS, WARSAW:

File 9-65-829
File 9-65-830
File 9-65-831
File 9-68-853

ARCHIVES OF THE POLISH INSTITUTE AND SIKORSKI MUSEUM, LONDON:

KOL 198 — Wawel Treasures:

Vol. 1 — Jozef A. Krzyda Polkowski, 1888-1981

Vol. 2 — History of Taking of Wawel Treasures to Canada

Vol. 3 — Inventory of Museum Objects/Wawel Treasures, 1940–57

Vol. 4 — Correspondence of Polkowski and Babinski — 1945, 1947–53

Vol. 5 — Correspondence between Gov't in London & Local
Authorities of Quebec

Vol. 6 — Financial Affairs, Reports and Preliminary Budgets

Vol. 7 — Correspondence of Aleksander Janta, 1951–59

Vol. 8 — Correspondence with Representatives of Polish Peoples'
Rep. and Private Persons

Vol. 9 — Various Topics

Vol. 10 — Photographs

Vol. 11 — Letters of Babinski

Vol. 12 — Babinski's Notes, 1949–57

Vol. 13 — Wawel Collection Financial Affairs, 1948–57

Vol. 14 — Adam Zurowski's Correspondence

Vol. 15 — Reports of Polkowski & His Financial Reports, 1957–61

Vol. 16 — Correspondence of Zurowski with London Government,
1957–60

Vol. 17 — Correspondence of Zurowski with Janta, 1957–60

Vol. 18 — Wawel Chests Stored in Bank of Montreal

Vol. 19 — The Return of Wawel Treasures to Poland, 1957–61 and earlier

Vol. 20 — Wawel/Articles from the Press

Vol. 21 — Press Cuttings II

Vol. 22 — Untitled

KOL 408 — Foreign Ministry / Canada:

Vol. 92 — 1954

Vol. 93 — 1955

Vol. 94 — 1956

Vol. 95 — 1957

Vol. 96 — 1958

Vol. 97 — 1959

Vol. 98 — 1960
Vol. 99 — 1961

SECONDARY SOURCES:

BOOKS:

Ros, J. *Tajennice Arrosowego Skarbu* (The Secret of the Wawel Treasures). Warsaw: KsiazkaWiedza, 1963.

Skuza, Cezarius. *Wojenne I Powojenne Losy Polskich Skarbow Narodowych* (Fate of the Polish National Treasures During and After the Second World War). Torun, 1994.

ARTICLES:

Kowecka, A. "Ochrona Zbiorow Biblioteki Narodowej" (How the Collection of the National Library was Secured), in *Walka o dobra Kultury, 1939–45*, vol. I: 179–242. Warsaw: Panstowy Institut Wydawniczy, 1970.

"Malcuzynski," in *Popularna Encyclopedia Powszechna* (Universal Popular Encyclopedia), Cracow, 1995.

Polkowski, Franciszek. "Park in Zelazowa Wola," *Chopin*, vol.1 (1937).

Wiorczynski, S. "Palladium Biblioteki Narodowej Uratowane" (The Most Precious Things of the National Library are Saved), *Odrodzenie*, KW III & IV (1947): 27–52.

NEWSPAPERS:

Glos Ludu (The Voice of the People)

Przekroj (Cross Cut)

Trybuna Ludu (The People's Tribune)

Zycie Warszawa (Warsaw Life)

There are many newspaper articles in the files of the Polish Institute and Sikorski Museum in London, as well as in those of the Ministry of Foreign Affairs in Warsaw. They consisted of reports from Polish papers as well as dispatches from Canadian newspapers sent from the Polish legation in Ottawa.

NOTES

AAN=Archives de l'Assemblée nationale, Québec, QC;

ANQ=Archives nationales du Québec, QC;

ASA=Archives de Soeurs Augustines, Hôtel Dieu, Québec, QC;

CI =Archives of Chopin Institute (Archivum Institut Frederyka Chopina), Warsaw, Poland;

MFAW=Archives of Ministry of Foreign Affairs (Archivum Ministerstvo Spraw Zagranicznych, Warsaw, Poland;

NAC=National Archives of Canada, Ottawa, ON;

NGC= National Gallery of Canada (Library and Archives), Ottawa, ON;

NLC=National Library of Canada, Ottawa, ON;

SI = Archives of Polish Institute and Sikorski Museum, London, UK

CHAPTER 1: THE STORM CLOUDS GATHER

1 Aloysius Balawyder, *The Odyssey of the Polish Art Treasures*, 7–8.
2 Adam Zamoyski, *The Polish Way*, 52, 90–91.
3 *Ibid.*, 40, 68, 70, 109.
4 *Ibid.*, 169–70.
5 *Ibid.*, 257, and a quotation from an article by J. Szablowski found in Balawyder, 25–26.
6 Stanisláw Lorenz, *Canada Refuses to Return Polish Cultural Treasures*, 9.
7 Zamoyski, 354.
8 Balawyder, 8.
9 Zamoyski, 35–36, and *Zycie Warsawa* (*Warsaw Life*), February 3, 1959.
10 Balawyder, 26.

11   *Ibid.*, 24, 33–34.
12   *Ibid.*, 24–26.
13   *Ibid.*, 26.
14   *Ibid.*, 7.

CHAPTER 2: ESCAPE

15   Polkowski's *Long Memoir*, 6. Found at NAC, MG-28, Vol. 79 (hereafter referred to as Polkowski LM).
16   Polkowski's *Short Memoir*, 1–3. Found in same place (and hereafter referred to as Polkowski SM).
17   Jerzy Petrus, "L'odysée des trésors polonais," in *Le retour des trésors polonais* (catalogue for an exposition at the Musée du Quebec in 2001), 27–28.
18   This description of Polkowski is based upon a studio portrait done in Paris in April 1940, found in the NAC Reference Section, Adam Zurowski Collection, accession number 1993-359. It is also based on descriptions of Polkowski during his early years in Canada in *The Globe and Mail*, November 8, 1946, and in an article by Mackenzie Porter, "Who's Going to Get the Polish Art Treasures?" in *Maclean's*, July 15, 1953.
19   Polkowski LM, 7–11, and Balawyder, 9–10.
20   The last comment in the description of Zaleski is mine. The rest of the description comes from Porter's article in *Maclean's*, July 15, 1953, 41–42.
21   Polkowski LM, 11–13, and Polkowski SM, 4.

CHAPTER 3: TOUGH DECISIONS

22   Polkowski LM, 14–15.
23   Polkowski SM, 5.
24   Polkowski LM, 16–19.
25   *Ibid.*, 6.
26   *Ibid.*, 19–23.
27   *Ibid.*, 23–27.
28   *Ibid.*, 28–29.
29   *Ibid.*, 29.

CHAPTER 4: FURTHER VOYAGING

30   Polkowski SM, 7.
31   Polkowski LM, 30.
32   Balawyder, 15.
33   Polkowski LM, 30.

34 Commentary by guide at Wawel Castle, 1993.

35 J. Ros, *Tajennice Arrosowego Skarbu*, 42–53, and Petrus article, 37.

36 Balawyder, 16–17.

37 Polkowski LM, 31.

38 Balawyder, 17. Balawyder places these events on the same dates as Polkowski, but in the month of October. Polkowski's November dates make more sense in view of the timing of the rest of the voyage.

39 Polkowski SM, 8.

40 Polkowski LM, 31.

41 *Ibid.*, 31–32.

42 *Ibid.*, 32–33.

43 *Ibid.*, 33.

44 *Ibid.*, 33.

45 Polkowski SM, 9.

46 Polkowski LM, 33.

47 *Ibid.*, 33–34.

CHAPTER 5: SOJOURN IN FRANCE

48 Statement of Stanisláw Swierz Zaleski re: the objects of art brought in 1940 for safekeeping in Canada, November 20, 1946, NAC RG 25, File #837-40, Vol. 2803 … 1.

49 Polkowski LM, 35, and Polkowski SM, 10.

50 Statement of Zaleski, November 20, 1946, 2–3.

51 Balawyder, 18.

52 Polkowski SM, 10.

53 Polkowski LM 5, 35, and Polkowski SM, 10.

54 Polkowski SM, 10.

55 Balawyder, 18–19.

56 Polkowski LM, 35–36.

57 *Ibid.*, 36.

58 Petrus article, 39.

59 J. Mazurkowa, "Engineer Jozef Krzyzda Polkowski, the Faithful Custodian of the Wawel Treasures," the Polish Historical Society in Great Britain's *Historical Papers*, Vol. 21, 294.

60 Polkowski LM, 36.

CHAPTER 6: ON THE ROAD AGAIN

61 Polkowski LM, 36–40.

62 Petrus article, 39–40 & Lorenz brochure, 10–11.

63 Lorenz, 11–12.

64 Interview with Mariola Nalecz, curator at the National Library Warsaw, August 2001.

65 A. Kowecka, "Ochrona Zbiorow Biblioteki Narodowej," *Walka O Dobra Kultury,1939–45*, Vol. I, 186; S. Wiorczynski, "Palladium Biblioteki Narodowej Uratowane," in *Odrodzenie*, 1947, KW III & IV, 27–52; and Cesarius Skuza, *Wojenne I Powojenne Losy Polskich Skarbow Narodowych.*

66 Polkowski LM, 40.

67 Polkowski LM, 41

68 *Ibid.*, 41, and report by Antoni Slonimski in *Trybuna Ludu*, January 8, 1961, NAC RG 25, File #837-40, Vol. 5022...16.

69 Polkowski LM, 42, and statement by Zaleski, November 20, 1946, page 3, NAC RG 25, File #837-40, Vol. 2803...1.

70 Polkowski LM, 42–43, 46.

71 *Ibid.*, 43, and Podoski's correspondence of June 24 and July 11, 1940, NAC RG 25, File #837-40, 2803...1.

72 Polkowski LM, 43, and Balawyder, 29.

73 Polkowski LM, 44–45

74 Polkowski LM, 45.

75 Podoski to External Affairs, July 11, 1940, NAC RG 25, File #837-40, 2803...1.

76 Polkowski LM, 45, and Polkowski SM, 13.

CHAPTER 7: CANADA — A SAFE HAVEN

77 T.D. Mitic, "Guarding The Gold," *The Beaver*, October-November 2000, 39–40.

78 L.F. Jackson to External Affairs, July 16, 1940, cited in Balawyder, 90.

79 Polkowski LM, 46–47.

80 Balawyder, 31.

81 Podoski to Lanctot, August 1, 1940, NAC RG 25, File #837-40, 2803...1.

82 Lanctot to Podoski, August 2, 1940, NAC RG 25, File #837-40, 2803...1.

83 Polkowski LM, 47.

84 Balawyder, 31, and Podoski to Public Works, July 27, 1940, cited in Balawyder, 90–91.

85 Polkowski LM, 47.

86 Balawyder, 35.

87 National Registration Certificate of Jozef Krzyda Polkowski, NAC RG 18, File #1946-HQ-1046-A-1, Vol. 6094...1.

88 National Registration Certificate of Stanisláw Swierz Zaleski, obtained at Census Operation Division, Statistics Canada.

89 Report of Polkowski and Zaleski to London government-in-exile, February 10, 1941, found at SI, KOL 198/5.

90 Balawyder, 31.

91 Report of Polkowski and Zaleski to London, February 10, 1941.

92 *Ibid.*

93 Balawyder, 34–35.

94 Kelly Egan, interviewing Ed Sliwka in "The Amazing Saga of Poland's Treasures," *Ottawa Citizen*, August 29, 1999.

95 Note by Z. Bielski, September 29, 1947, sent to External Affairs by Sieradski, November 12, 1954, NAC RG 25, File #837-40, Vol. 6769...10.1.

96 Inventory list of Polish treasures, SI, KOL 198/9.

97 Report of Polkowski and Zaleski to London, February 10, 1941.

98 Report of Polkowski and Zaleski to London, February 13, 1942, SI, KOL 198/5.

99 Inventory list of Polish treasures, SI, KOL 198/9.

100 Polkowski LM, 47.

101 Report of Polkowski & Zaleski to London, 10 February 1941.

102 Report of September 1943, SI, KOL 198/6.

103 Statement by Zaleski, November 20, 1946, p.4 NAC RG 25, File #837-40. Vol. 2803...1, and Balawyder, 32.

104 Polkowski SM, 15–16.

105 Report of September 1943, SI, KOL 198/6; also *Catalogue for Exhibition of Polish Art* and many news clippings, NGC, File 1942 — Polish Art, exhibitions and documentation file.

CHAPTER 8: THE FORTUNES OF WAR

106 Zamoyski, 356–57.

107 *Ibid.*, 357.

108 *Ibid.*, 357–58.

109 *Ibid.*, 359.

110 *Ibid.*, 359–60.

111 *Ibid.*, 364–68.

112 *Ibid.*, 359, 362–63.

113 *Ibid.*, 364, 369.

114 Balawyder, 38.

115 Report on the Yalta Conference, as quoted in A. Balawyder, *The Odyssey of the Polish Treasures*, 45–46.

116 Zamoyski, 369.

117 Balawyder, 46–47.

Chapter 9: Missing Treasures

118 *L'Action Catholique*, March 3, 1948.

119 Egan article, Ottawa *Citizen*, August 29, 1999.

120 *Time*, November 18, 1946.

121 Balawyder, 47.

122 *Ibid.*, 47–48.

123 J. Polkowski, *How the Treasure Was Hidden*, 8. Found at SI, KOL 198/2.

124 Balawyder, 48. Also "Polish Art Collection in Canada — Historic Background." a September 6, 1949, draft report found at NAC RG 25, File #837-40, 6182...5.2. Also Polkowski, *How the Treasure Was Hidden*, 8.

125 Balawyder, 38.

126 *Ibid.*, 38–39. Also, a description of Babinski's career written by himself, undated, found at SI, KOL 198/12.

127 Balawyder, 39–40, & Polkowski LM, 49.

128 Balawyder, 40–41. Confirmed by "Notes sur les trésors polonais," a document initialled by Archbishop Roy and sent to Duplessis, January 20, 1959, ANQ, P688, S3, SS9 / 367, and by a report in *Le Devoir*, June 5, 1958.

129 Statement by Zaleski, November 20, 1946, 7–8, NAC RG 25, File #837-40, Vol. 2803...1.

Chapter 10: The Canadian Response

130 Balawyder, 49.

131 Riddell to Robertson, January 26, 1946, NAC RG 25, File #9396-40, Vol. 3912...1.

132 Comment by Robertson on memo from H.F.C., April 5, 1946, NAC RG 25, File #837-40, Vol. 2803...1.

133 Beaudry to External Affairs, May 16, 1946, *Ibid.*

134 Balawyder, 32.

135 Molson to Riddell, January 28 and January 30, 1946, NAC RG 25, File #837-40, Vol. 2803...1.

136 Riddell to Robertson, February 2, 1946, *Ibid.*

137 Carter to Robertson, April 12, 1946, *Ibid.*

138 Comment by Robertson on memo from Carter, April 5, 1946, *Ibid.*

139 Wrong to Public Works, May 17, 1946, *Ibid.*

140 Zanek to Wood, June 4, 1946, NAC RG 18, File #1946-HQ-1046-A-1, Vol. 6094...1.

CHAPTER 11: THE SEARCH

141 Semil to Ministry of Culture, October 4, 1946, MFAW, File 9-65-829.

142 Polkowski, *How the Treasure Was Hidden*, 8–9. This visit to Quebec City took place between May 23 and June 2.

143 Beaudry to Robertson, May 16, 1946, NAC RG 25, File #837-40, Vol. 2803...1.

144 J.A. McC. to Wrong, May 18 and May 20, 1946, *Ibid.*

145 Wrong to Escott Reid, May 17, 1946, *Ibid.*

146 Three letters by External Affairs, May 22–25, 1946, *Ibid.*

147 Three letters to External Affairs, May 27, May 29 and May 31, 1946, NAC RG 25, File #837-40, Vol. 6771...1.

148 Polkowski, *How the Treasure Was Hidden*, 6.

149 *Ibid.*, 7–9. And, for Cardinal Villeneuve's involvement, Wood to Ilsley, February 4, 1948, NAC RG 25, File #837-40, Vol. 3555...3.

150 Polish Legation to External Affairs, June 21, 1946, NAC RG 25, File #837-40, Vol. 2803...1.

151 Wrong to Fiderkiewicz, August 2, 1946, *Ibid.*

152 Wrong to Polish Legation, August 23, 1946, MFAW, File 9-65-829.

153 Fiderkiewicz to Ministry of Foreign Affairs, August 21, 1946, with inventory enclosed, *Ibid.*

154 Letters found at NAC RG 25, File #837-40, Vol. 2803...1 and MFAW, File 9-65-829.

155 Report to Officer Commanding, "A" Division, RCMP, May 30, 1946, NAC RG 18, File #1946-HQ-1046-A-1, Vol. 6094...1.

156 Ibid.

157 Polkowski LM, 51.

158 Polkowski, *How the Treasure Was Hidden*, 9.

159 Report of C.H. Bayfield re: Stanislas Swierz Zaleski, June 20, 1946, NAC RG 25, File # 837-40, Vol. 2803 ...1.

160 *Ibid.*

161 Polish Legation to External Affairs, July 2, 1946, *Ibid.*

162 Bayfield, *Ibid.*

CHAPTER 12: QUESTIONS ASKED

163 Ottawa *Journal*, November 7, 1946: 1, 6

164 Ottawa *Journal*, November 8, 1946: 17.

165 *Ibid.*

166 Ottawa *Journal*, November 9, 1946: 26.

167 *L'Humanité*, November 9, 1946, found with report from Canadian Embassy in Paris, November 15, 1946, NAC RG 25, File #837-40, Vol. 2803…1.

168 *Arts*, November 22, 1946, included with report from Canadian Embassy to Pearson, November 25, 1946, *Ibid.*

169 H.H. Wrong, internal memo for department, November 12, 1946, *Ibid.*

170 Press release from External Affairs, November 12, 1946, *Ibid.*

171 Memo by Pearson re: interview with Polkowski and Brockington, November 16, 1946, *Ibid.*

172 Memo by R.G. Riddell for External Affairs, November 22, 1946; Robertson to Pearson, May 29, 1947; External Affairs to St. Laurent, 8 April 1947; and Canadian Consulate in New York to External Affairs, September 25, 1947; all found at NAC RG 25, File #837-40. Vol. 2803…1.

CHAPTER 13: A BIRD IN THE HAND

173 Zamoyski, 370.

174 Bielski to Fiderkiewicz re: impending departure of latter, July 12, 1947, MFAW, File 9-65-830.

175 *L'Action Catholique*, March 3, 1948.

176 Memo from R.G. Riddell, December 26, 1946, NAC RG 25, File #837-40, Vol. 2803…1.

177 St. Laurent to Ilsley, December 2, 1947; Ilsley to St. Laurent, December 5, 1947; Regan of CIB Ottawa to Officer Commanding "A" Division, RCMP, December 5, 1947; all found at NAC RG 18, File #1946-HQ-1046-A-1, Vol. 6094…1.

178 Unsigned note on House of Commons Press Gallery stationery, marked private, March 8, 1948, NAC RG 25, File #837-40, Vol. 3555…3.

179 Report of Mother St. Henri written in January 1961, ASA, Les trésors polonais, tiroir 11-C960. Also, Balawyder, 54–55 and memo for St. Laurent, February 14, 1948, NAC RG 25, File #837-40, Vol. 3555…3.

180 Wood to Ilsley, January 30, 1948, NAC RG 18, File #1946-HQ-1046-A-1, Vol. 6094…1.

181 Pearson to Bielski, February 13, 1948, *Ibid.*

182 Report of Mother St. Henri, January 1961, ASA, tiroir 11-C960.

183 Bielski to St. Henri, February 21, 1948, ANQ, Conseil executif, 03Q-E5, File 2 C 030 04-06-004B-01/2.1.

184 Babinski to St. Henri, February 23, 1948, ASA, tiroir 11-C960.

CHAPTER 14: A BIRD IN THE BUSH

185 *Questions re: Polish Art Treasures*, NAC RG 18, File #1946-HQ-1046-A-1, Vol. 6094...2, p.195.

186 Report of Mother St. Henri, January 1961, ASA, tiroir 11-C960.

187 Wood to Ilsley, February 27, 1948, NAC RG 18, #1946-HQ-1046-A-1, Vol. 6094...2, p.102.

188 Wood to Ilsley, March 2, 1948, *Ibid.*, 103.

189 BUP dispatch, found in Ottawa *Journal*, March 3, 1948.

190 *Ibid.*

191 Declaration by Mother St. Henri, quoted by St. Laurent in House of Commons, March 4, 1948, NAC RG 25, File #837-40, Vol. 3555...3. The statement that Babinski ordered the removal of the treasures to the Provincial Museum is corroborated in her letter to Premier Duplessis, February 25, 1948, ANQ, File P688, S3, SS9/367.

192 The statement of Commissioner Wood as reported verbatim in the House of Commons by the Secretary of State for External Affairs, March 4, 1948. Found at NAC RG 25, #837-40, 3555...3

193 St. Henri to Duplessis, requesting help, February 25, 1948, NAC RG 25, File 837-B-40, Vol. 6771...3.2.

194 St. Henri to Duplessis thanking him, February 25, 1948, quoted in the Ottawa *Journal*, 3 March 1948.

CHAPTER 15: THE PREMIER OF QUEBEC

195 Campaign speech by Maurice Duplessis, June 17, 1934. Quoted in Conrad Black, *Duplessis*, 74.

196 Black, 447–448.

197 *Ibid.*, 500–501, 578.

198 *Ibid.*, 592, 611–12.

199 Duplessis to J.W. McConnell, August 6, 1951. Quoted in Black, 608.

CHAPTER 16: POLITICAL MANOEUVRING

200 Newspaper clipping (source unknown) containing an interview with Walter Duchesnay at the time of the treasures' departure from the Provincial Museum in Quebec on January 2, 1961, ASA, tiroir 11-C960. The name and date of the newspaper are missing.

201 *Ottawa Journal*, March 4, 1948.

202 Statement by St. Laurent in House of Commons, March 4, 1948, NAC RG 25, File #837-40, Vol. 3555...3.

203 BUP dispatch, March 5, 1948, NAC RG 25, File #837-40, Vol. 3555...3.

204 *L'Action Catholique*, March 10, 1948 in Archives nationales du Quebec, File # P688, S3, SS9, #367 Trésors polonais.

205 *Saturday Night*, March 13, 1948.

206 Memo for St. Laurent, September 14, 1948, NAC RG 25, File #837-40, Vol. 3555...4. Also, Petrus article, 43.

207 *La Presse*, September 25, 1948.

208 Memo for St. Laurent, September 14, 1948, NAC RG 25, File #837-40, Vol. 3555...4.

CHAPTER 17: INTERNATIONAL REPERCUSSIONS

209 Zamoyski, 370–71, 374–75.

210 Kirkwood to Pearson, March 7, 1948, NAC RG 25, File #837-40, Vol. 3555...3.

211 *Przekroj*, December 5–11, 1948, found at NAC RG 25, File #837-40, Vol. 3555...4

212 *Gros Ludu* (The Voice of the People), December 6, 1948, found at NAC RG 25, File #837-40, Vol. 3555...4.

213 Kirkwood to Pearson, March 3, 1949, *Ibid.*

214 Balawyder, 62.

215 Kirkwood to External Affairs, February 17, 1949, NAC RG 25, File #837-40, Vol. 3555...4.

216 Kirkwood to External Affairs, March 1, 1949, *Ibid.*

217 External Affairs to Canadian Delegation to UNESCO, October 1, 1956, reviewing discussions at UN re: Polish treasures since 1949, NAC RG 25, File #837-40, Vol. 6769...9.1.

218 Dr. Stanisláw Lorenz, *Canada Refuses to Return Polish Cultural Treasures*, 7.

219 Lorenz brochure, 9–14, 75–84.

220 Balawyder, 65–66, and External Affairs to RCMP, February 27, 1950, NAC RG 18, File #1946-HQ-1046-A-1, Vol. 6094...2.

221 Polish delegation at UN to all heads of delegations, December 1, 1949, NAC RG 25, File #837-40, Vol. 6182...5.2.

CHAPTER 18: CARE TAKING

222 Inventory of eight trunks stored at Convent of Precious Blood enclosed with Bayfield's report of December 31, 1947, NAC, RG 18, File 1946-HQ-1046-A-1, Vol. 6094...1.

223 Memo from Macdonnell to Minister of External Affairs, May 1, 1956, NAC RG 25, File #837-40, Vol. 6769...8.2.

224 Report of RCMP, January 15, 1951, NAC RG 25, File #837-40, Vol. 6182...5.1.

225 Memo by Kirkwood of External Affairs, March 29, 1951, *Ibid.*

226 Babinski to Antoine Roy, October 13, 1948, as found at ANQ, E53, v. 1919-00-006/57.

227 Babinski to Roy, November 10, 1948, NAC RG 25, File #837-40, Vol. 6182...5.1

228 Porter, John: "De Cracovie à Québec...," article in *Le retour des trésors polonais*, 18.

229 Interview with Polkowski in *Glas Polski*, Toronto, date unknown, quoted verbatim in *Dziennek Chicagowski*, December 9, 1957, NAC RG 25, File #837-40, Vol. 6770...11.2. Also, report from Polkowski to Babinski, June 23, 1948, SI, Kol 198/12.

230 Report Polkowski to Babinski, June 23, 1948, *Ibid.*

231 Reports by Polkowski, February 18 and November 12, 1952, *Ibid.*

232 Report by Polkowski, April 17, 1955, *Ibid.*

233 Porter article in *Le retour des trésors polonais*, 15. Also, report of Polkowski, October 3, 1953, found at SI, KOL 198/12.

234 *Maclean's*, 15 December 1953, pp. 14, 17, found at NAC RG 25, File #837-40, 6341...6.2

235 Report of Polkowski, October 3, 1953, found at SI, KOL 198/12.

236 Report of Polkowski, 2 November 1953, *Ibid.*

237 December 15, 1953, for *Maclean's* and December 14, 1953, for *Life* magazine.

238 This committee was established by July 9, 1945, according to information found at NAC RG 25, File #9396-40, Vol. 3912...1.

239 Polkowski and Zaleski to F. Frankowski, October 25, 1945, and the same to another minister, perhaps Wiktor Podoski, October 29, 1945, SI, KOL 198/6.

240 Zurowski to Duplessis, September 23, 1957, SI, KOL 198/4.

241 Babinski to Duplessis, January 17, 1949, ANQ, no further information.

242 Babinski to Roy, November 10, 1948, found at Archives nationales du Quebec, File ANQ-Q, E53, v. 1919-00-006 / 57

243 Polkowski & Zaleski to Babinski, August 23, 1945, SI, KOL 198/4.

244 Polkowski & Zaleski to Frankowski, October 25, 1945, and to another minister, October 29, 1945, SI, KOL 198/6.

245 Podoski's letter, November 6, 1945, quoted in Dr. Zaleski's statement of 1946 re the Polish treasures, found at NAC RG 25, File # 837-40, Vol. 2803...1

246 Memo Riddell to Robertson, 26 January 1946, NAC RG 25, File #9396-40, Vol. 3912...1.

247 Polish Legation to External Affairs, 2 July 1946, NAC RG 25, File

#837-40, Vol. 2803…1.

248 Polkowski SM, 15.

249 Polkowski SM 16.

250 Two letters from Polkowski to London government-in-exile, April 7 & 30, 1947, SI, KOL 198/1.

251 Polkowski to Huston, November 29, 1957, SI, KOL 198/1.

252 *Ibid.* Also J. Mazurkowa, "Engineer Jozef Krzyda Polkowski, the Faithful Custodian of the Wawel Treasures" in Polish Historical Society in Great Britain's *Historical Papers*, Vol. 21, 297.

253 Babinski to Roy, October 7, 1949, ANQ, Conseil executif, O3Q:E5, trésors polonais.

254 Zurowski to Babinski, November 1, 1951, SI, KOL 198/12.

255 Polkowski to Babinski, November 12, 1951, at SI, KOL 198/12

256 Polkowski to Babinski, December 28, 1951, *Ibid.*

257 Two letters from Polkowski to Babinski, October 15, 1953 & June 23, 1954, SI, KOL 198/12.

258 Memo from Pick to Under-secretary of State for External Affairs, May 26, 1958, NAC RG 25, File #837-40, Vol. 6770…11.1, and Polkowski SM 16.

259 Photo in Adam Zurowski Collection, NAC Refernce Section, #1993-359.

260 Interview with Alfred Zurowski, the son of Adam Zurowski, in Kelly Egan's *Ottawa Citizen* article, August 29, 1999.

261 Mazurkowa article, 301.

262 Polkowski to Babinski, February 2, 1954, SI, KOL 198/12.

263 Polkowski to Babinski, May 18, 1954, *Ibid.*

264 Memo from Pick to Under-secretary of State for External Affairs, May 26, 1958, NAC RG 25, File #837-40, Vol. 6770…11.1.

265 M. Salter and G. McLachlan, *Poland: The Rough Guide*, 101–104. Also, article by F. Polkowski, "Park in Zelazowa Wola," in booklet *Chopin*, Vol. I, 1937.

266 J. Zaleska, *Franciszek Krzyda Polkowski, 1881–1949*, unpublished memoir found in the archives of Chopin Institute, Warsaw.

267 Mazurkowa article, 299, and letter from Committee of National Treasures in Canada to Anders group in London, July 13, 1956, SI, KOL 198/12.

268 Three letters Polkowski to Babinski, September 24, October 10, November 25, 1956, *Ibid.*

CHAPTER 19: CONFRONTATION AGAIN

269 Note from Polish Ministry of Foreign Affairs to Canadian legation, Warsaw, March 25, 1952, NAC RG 25, File #837-40, Vol. 6341…6.1.

270 The letter from the Warsaw university professors was reproduced in the newspaper *Trybuna Ludu* on November 1, 1955, and the one from the Jagiellonian University in Cracow to Pearson was written on October 24, 1955. All these documents are found at NAC RG 25, File #837-40, Vol. 6769...8.1.

271 Reports of Polkowski to Babinski, October 27, 1954, April 17, 1955, and October 18, 1955, SI, KOL 198/12.

272 "The Saved Treasures," article by Cat, January 5, 1961, NAC RG25, File #837-40, Vol. 5022...16. Also, article by M Kasprzycki in *Przekroj*, March 20, 1955, NAC RG 25, File #837-40, Vol. 6341...7.1.

273 *Zycie Warszawy*, April 3–4, 1955, NAC RG 25, File #837-40, Vol. 6341...7.2.

274 "How Much Longer...?" in *Zycie Warszawy*, November 2–3, 1958, NAC RG 25, File #837-40, Vol. 6770...12.1

275 Polkowski to Babinski, April 17, 1955, SI, KOL 198/12.

276 Memo from Canadian ambassador to Spain to External Affairs, October 5, 1959, NAC RG 25, File #837-40, Vol. 6770...13. Also, article in *Zycie Warszawy*, February 28–29, 1960, NAC RG 25, File #837-40, Vol. 6771...13.2.

Chapter 20: Détente

277 Zamoyski: *The Polish Way*, 377-80.

278 Zurowski to London government-in-exile, December 19, 1957, SI, KOL 198/19.

279 Memo from T. Sypniewski (senior producer of Polish section of CBC's International Service) to External Affairs, May 27, 1958, NAC RG 25, File #837-40, Vol. 6770...11.1.

280 Memo from Secretary of State for External Affairs to Prime Minister, March 7, 1957, NAC RG 25, File #837-40, Vol. 6769...9.1.

281 Resolution of Canadian Polish Congress, October 11–13, 1958, SI, KOL 198/19.

282 Stanisław Babinski, the son of Dr. W. Babinski, to Château Group of London Poles, August 12, 1957, SI, KOL 198/12.

283 Polkowski LM, 53–54 & Polkowski report to Babinski, February 12, 1957, SI, KOL 198/12.

284 Polkowski to Babinski, February 12, 1957, Sikorski Institute, KOL 198/12

285 Polkowski LM, 54.

286.A. McCordick to Charles Ritchie, September 24, 1952, NAC RG 25, File #837-40, Vol. 6341...6.1.

287 Memo Legal Division to M.H. Warshof, September 3, 1954, NAC

RG 25, File #837-40, Vol. 6341…7.1.

288 Memo from T.L. Carter to J.A. McCordick re: legal position of Polish treasures, February 25, 1952, NAC RG 25, File #837-40, Vol. 6341…6.1.

289 *Le Devoir*, January 17, 1956.

290 Report "Vows Reds Won't Get Treasures" in Montreal *Star*, January 17, 1958, NAC RG 25, File #837-40, Vol. 6769…10.2.

291 Inventory of articles stored at Bank of Montreal by Polkowski, November 19, 1946, NAC RG 25, File #837-40, Vol. 6770…10 FP1.1.

292 Documents submitted by Polish Legation, September 18, 1957, NAC RG 25, File #837-40, Vol. 6769…10.1.

293 Memo from Pearson to Cabinet, August 7, 1956, NAC RG 25, File #837-40, Vol. 6769…8.2.

294 *Ottawa Citizen*, September 5, 1957, NAC RG 25, File #837-40, Vol. 6769…10.1.

295 Memo A.J. Pick to Under Secretary of State for External Affairs, 26 May 1958, NAC RG 25, File #837-40, Vol. 6770…11.1.

296 Memo from Pick to Undersecretary of State for External Affairs, May 29, 1958, *Ibid.*

297 The Minutes for this meeting of the Standing Committee on External Affairs were found at the Sikorski Institute, KOL 198/18.

CHAPTER 21: A MUSICAL INTERLUDE

298 References to Witold Malcuzynski (1914–1977) are from *New Grove Dictionary of Music and Musicians* and *Popularna Encyclopedia Powszechna* (Universal Popular Encyclopedia).

299 All three of these interviews are described in Polkowski LM, 54–55.

300 *Ibid.*, 56.

301 Telegram from the Canadian legation in Warsaw to External Affairs, November 25, 1958, NAC RG 25, File #837-40, Vol. 6770…12.1.

302 Department of Citizenship and Immigration to Robertson, November 28, 1958, *Ibid.*

303 Memo from Robertson to D. Fulton, Minister of Justice, September 23, 1960, NAC RG 25, File #837-40, Vol. 5022…14.

304 *Ibid.*, and Polkowski LM, 57.

305 Polkowski LM, 56–57.

306 J.W. Holmes to Acting Minister of External Affairs, December 10, 1958, NAC RG 25, File #837-40, Vol. 6770…12.1.

307 Ivan Sabourin to Premier Antonio Barette of Quebec, January 18, 1960, ANQ, 03Q-E5 (#2 C 030 04-06-004B-01) / 2.1 Trésors polonais.

308 Zurowski to Pajac, December 16, 1958, SI, KOL 198/16.

309 Memo from Robertson to D. Fulton, September 23, 1960, NAC RG 25, File #837-40, Vol. 5022...14.

310 Memo from J.W. Holmes to Acting Minister of External Affairs, December 18, 1958, NAC RG 25, File #837-40, Vol. 6770...12.1.

311 Polkowski LM, 57.

312 *Ibid.*, 57.

313 The information regarding the opening of the two trunks is found in Polkowski LM, 58, and in the protocol issued at the release of the trunks found in Appendix B, item 2 of Balawyder's *The Odyssey of the Polish Treasures*, 93–96.

314 Protocol from meeting of Executive Committee of Wawel Treasures Fund in New York, January 27, 1959, SI, KOL 198/17.

315 This interview with Alfred Zurowski was obtained by Kelly Egan for an article in the Ottawa *Citizen*, August 29, 1999.

316 Balawyder, 96–97 (Appendix B, items 3, 4 & 5).

317 Zurowski to Starzewski in London, February 12, 1959, SI, KOL 198/19.

318 "Polish Art Treasure Stops Here," Toronto *Telegram*, January 20, 1959. Also, Zurowski to Starzewski, February 12, 1959, SI, KOL 198/19.

319 Two RCMP reports dated January 15 & 22, 1959, NAC RG 18, File #1946-HQ-1046-A-1, Vol. 6094...3.

320 "On Their Way Home," *Trybuna Ludu*, January 21, 1959, NAC RG 25, File #837-40, Vol. 6770...12.2.

321 Telegram quoted in *Zycie Warszawy* (Warsaw Life), January 29, 1959, NAC RG 25, File #837-40, Vol. 6770...12.2

322 Dispatch in *Trybuna Ludu*, January 28, 1959, NAC RG 25, File #837-40, Vol. 6770...12.2.

323 Balawyder, 75.

324 *Trybuna Ludu*, January 11, 1959, NAC RG 25, File #837-40, Vol. 6770...12.1

325 *Trybuna Ludu*, February 8, 1959, NAC RG 25, File #837-40, Vol. 6770...12.2.

326 Balawyder, 76.

327 Information found in articles in *Trybuna Ludu*, February 15, 1959; *Polish Facts and Figures* (issued by press office of Polish embassy in London), February 21, 1959; and *New York Times*, February 17, 1959. All of these were found at NAC RG 25, File #837-40, Vol. 6770...12.2.

CHAPTER 22: THE END OF THE AFFAIR

328 The communications from Dr. Szablowski on May 11, 1959; from Dr. Morelowski on April 15 and May 9, 1959; and from Dr. Drzewiecki on

May 2, 1959, are all found at SI, KOL 198/8.

329 Halina Grabowska to Jozef Polkowski, February 15, 1959, SI, KOL 198/21.

330 J. Szablowski: brochure entitled *The Odyssey of the National Treasures*, 1-14. Also, H. Southam to External Affairs, August 26, 1960, NAC RG 25, File #837-40, Vol. 5022…14.

331 *Trybuna Ludu*, January 11, 1959, NAC RG 25, File #837-40, Vol. 6770…12.1

332 Polish Legation to External Affairs, September 10, 1959, NAC RG 25, File #837-40, Vol. 6770…13.1; Polish academics to Premier Barette, February 1, 1960, ANQ, File P688, S3, SS9 #367, Trésors polonais; Robertson to Minister of Ext. Aff. re Canadian Polish Congress, November 24, 1959, NAC RG 25, File #837-40, Vol. 6771…13.2.

333 Report by Dobell of External Affairs re: views of Podoski, June 12, 1959, NAC RG 25, File #837-40, Vol. 6770…12.2.

334 Conrad Black, *Duplessis*, 585, 587, 682–87.

335 *Ibid.*, 690.

336 Balawyder, 80 and 100–101 (Appendix C, Item 6).

337 Sabourin to Barette, February 18 and 29, 1960, ANQ, Conseil executif, 03Q-E5 (#2C 030 04-06-004B-01/2.1) Trésors polonais.

338 Zurowski to Executive Group, London, January 30, 1960, and Malcuzynski to Zurowski, February 24, 1960, both found at SI, KOL 198/19.

339 Malcuzynski to Zurowski, April 6, 1960, SI, KOL 198/19.

340 Cited in Balawyder, 99–100 (Appendix C).

341 Montreal *Gazette*, July 26, 1960, NAC RG 25, File #837-40, Vol. 5022…14.

342 Memo from A.J. Andrews to Robertson, August 24, 1960, NAC RG 25, File #837-40, Vol. 5022…14.

343 Two memos from Robertson, to Minister of External Affairs and to Prime Minister, October 27 and 28, 1960, NAC RG 25, File #837-40, Vol. 5022…14.

344 Telegram from External Affairs to Canadian legation in Warsaw, November 4, 1960, NAC RG 25, File #837-40, Vol. 5022…15.

345 Memo from Robertson to Minister of External Affairs, November 10, 1960, NAC RG 25, File #837-40, Vol. 5022…15. Also, memo from European Division of External Affairs entitled "The Return of the Polish Treasures," February 23, 1961, NAC RG 25, File #837-40, Vol. 5022…16, para.11.

346 Robertson to Minister of External Affairs, November 28, 1960, NAC RG 25, File #837-40, Vol. 5022…15, and Petrus article, 47.

347 Zurowski to Executive Group, London, December 14, 1960, SI, KOL 198/19, and Polkowski LM, 60.

348 Zurowski to Executive Group, London, December 23, 1960, SI, KOL 198/14.

349 Polkowski LM, 60–62.

350 Balawyder, 102 (Appendix C, Item #7), and Zurowski to Executive Group, London, January 4, 1961, SI, KOL 198/19.

CHAPTER 23: THE HOMECOMING

351 Report of RCMP, Quebec detachment, January 4, 1961, NAC, RG 18, File #1946 HQ 1046-A-1, Vol. 6094…3, and Montreal *Star*, January 3, 1961, NAC RG 25, File #837-40, Vol. 5022…16.

352 Memo from H.J. Davis to Minister of External Affairs, January 3, 1961, NAC RG 25, File #837-40, Vol. 5022…16.

353 *Ottawa Journal*, January 4, 1961, at NAC RG 18, File #1946 HQ 1046-A-1, Vol. 6094… 3.

354 *Trybuna Ludu*, January 5, 1961, *Ibid.*

355 Two radio interviews reported in *Zycie Warszawy*, January 7 and 10, 1961, *Ibid.*

356 Report of Peter Scott to G. H. Southam, January 18, 1961, NAC RG 25, File #837-40, Vol. 5022…16.

357 "Wawel Treasures Already in the Capital," *Trybuna Ludu*, January 17, 1961, found in long series of reports from Polish papers at NAC RG 25, File #837-40, Vol. 5022…16.

358 An interview given by Professors Szablowski and Marconi entitled "The Condition of the Wawel Treasures Does Not Evoke Any Fears," reported in *Zycie Warszawy*, January 18, 1961, *Ibid.*

359 *Trybuna Ludu*, January 7, 1961, found at NAC RG 25, File #837-40, Vol. 5022…16.

360 Introduction to Polkowski LM, 1.

361 Szablowski to Polkowski, December 12, 1959, SI, KOL 198/8.

362 Report by Southam to External Affairs, February 17, 1961, NAC RG 25, File #837-40, Vol. 5022…16. The report was written by Southam but submitted by P. Charpentier.

363 *Ibid.*

364 All of the information about the exhibition at the National Museum in Warsaw comes from the above report dated February 17, 1961.

365 Southam to External Affairs, March 24, 1961, found at NAC RG 25, File #837-40, Vol. 5022…16.

366 All of the information about the Wawel reception comes from Southam's report to External Affairs, March 24, 1961, NAC RG 25, File #837-40, Vol. 5022…16.

367 Southam to External Affairs, January 12, 1961, *Ibid.*

368 Memo from European Division of External Affairs, February 7, 1961, *Ibid.*

CHAPTER 24: POSTLUDE

369 In a letter dated March 17, 1961, Mr. Romer argued that Polkowski should not accept this kind of assistance. There were other voices of dissent and, in the long run, even Polkowski's friend Adam Zurowski advised him not to accept the Polish government's offer (Zurowski to Executive Group, London, April 14, 1961). Both letters are found at SI, KOL 198/19.

370 Zurowski to Executive Group, March 23, 1961, *Ibid.*

371 Article in *Zwiazkowiec*, Toronto, April 22, 1961, NAC RG 25, File #837-40, Vol. 5022...16, and comments by Andrew Garlicki to Kelly Egan in *Ottawa Citizen* article, August 29, 1999.

372 Polkowski LM, 62.

373 Polkowski SM, 16–17, as well as Polkowski's report *How the Treasure Was Hidden*, SI, KOL 198/2.

374 Polkowski SM, 15–16, and Egan article in *Ottawa Citizen*, August 19, 1999.

375 Obituary in *Ottawa Citizen*, October 13, 1981.

376 Petrus article, 44–45, and an interview with Dr. Petrus in August 2001.

377 Court decision re: Zaleski's property, April 17, 1953, NAC RG 25, File #837-40, Vol. 6769...10.1.

378 Le bulletin du Musée DuQuebec, printemps 2001, p.3.